The Intelligence of Woman

by W. L. George

CONTENTS

CHAPTER

I

THE INTELLIGENCE OF WOMAN

1

Men have been found to deny woman an intellect; they have credited her with instinct, with intuition, with a capacity to correlate cause and effect much as a dog connects its collar with a walk. But intellect in its broadest sense, the capacity consecutively to plan and steadfastly to execute, they have often denied her.

The days are not now so dark. Woman has a place in the state, a place under, but still a place. Man has recognized her value without coming to understand her much better, and so we are faced with a paradox: while man accords woman an improved social position, he continues to describe her as illogical, petty, jealous, vain, untruthful, disloyal to her own sex; quite as frequently he charges her with being over-loyal to her own sex: there is no pleasing him. Also he discerns in this unsatisfactory creature extreme unselfishness, purity, capacity for self-sacrifice. It seems that the intelligence of man cannot solve the problem of woman, which is a bad sign in a superior intelligence. The trouble lies in this: man assumes too readily that woman essentially differs from man. Hardly a man has lived who did not so exaggerate. Nietzsche, Schopenhauer, agreed to despise women; Napoleon seemed to view them as engines of pleasure; for Shakespeare they may well have embodied a romantic ideal, qualified by sportive wantonness. In Walter Scott, women appear as romance in a cheap edition; Byron in their regard is a beast of prey, Doctor Johnson a pompous brute and a puritanical sensualist. Cervantes mixed in his romantic outlook a sort of suspicious hatred, while Alexandre Dumas thought them born only to lay laurel wreaths and orange blossoms (together with coronets) on the heads of musketeers. All, all--from Thackeray, who never laid his hand upon a woman save in the way of patronage, to Goethe, to Dante, to Montaigne, to Wellington--all harbored this curious idea: in one way or another woman differs from man. And to-day, whether we read Mr. Bernard Shaw, Mr. George Moore, M. Paul Bourget, or Mr. Hall Caine, we find that there still persists a belief in Byron's lines:--

"What a strange thing is man! And what a stranger Is woman!"

Almost every man, except the professional Lovelace (and he knows nothing), believes in the mystery of woman. I do not. For men are also mysterious to women; women are quite as puzzled by our stupidity as by our subtlety. I do not believe that there is either a male or a female mystery; there is only the mystery of mankind. There are to-day differences between the male and the female intellect; we have to ask ourselves whether they are absolute or only apparent, or whether they are absolute but removable by education and time, assuming this to be desirable. I believe that these differences are superficial, temporary, traceable to hereditary and local influences. I believe that they will not endure forever, that they will tend to vanish as environment is modified, as old suggestions cease to be made.

This leads us to consider present idiosyncrasies in woman as a sex, her apparently low and apparently high impulses, her exaltations, and, in the light of her achievements, her future. I do not want to generalize hastily. The subject is too complex and too obscure for me to venture so to do, and I would ask my readers to remember throughout this chapter that I am not laying down the law, but trying only to arrive at the greatest possible frequency of truth. This is a short research of tendencies. There are human tendencies, such as belief in a divine spirit, painting pictures, making war, composing songs. Are there any special female tendencies? Given that we glimpse what distinguishes man from the beast, is there anything that distinguishes woman from man? In the small space at my disposal I cannot pretend to deal extensively with the topic. One reason is the difficulty of securing true evidence. Questions addressed to women do not always yield the truth; nor do questions addressed to men; for a desire to please, vanity, modesty, interfere. But the same question addressed to a woman may, according to circumstances, be sincerely answered in four ways,--

1. Truthfully, with a defensive touch, if she is alone with another woman.

2. With intent to cause male rivalry if she is with two men.

3. With false modesty and seductive evasiveness if she is with one man and one woman.

4. With a clear intention to repel or attract if she is with a man alone.

And there are variations of these four cases! A man investigating woman's points of view often finds the response more emotional than intellectual. Owing to the system under which we live, where man is a valuable prey, woman has contracted the habit of trying to attract. Even aggressive insolence on her part may conceal the desire to attract by exasperating. These notes must, therefore, be taken only as hints, and the reader may be interested to know that they are based on the observation of sixty-five women, subdivided as follows: Intimate acquaintance, five; adequate acquaintance, nineteen; slight acquaintance, forty-one; married, thirty-nine; status uncertain, eight; celibate, eighteen. Ages, seventeen to sixty-eight (average age, about thirty-five).

2

It is most difficult to deduce the quality of woman's intellect from her conduct, because her impulses are frequently obscured by her policy. The physical circumstances of her life predispose her to an interest in sex more dominant than is the case with man. As intellect flies out through the window when emotion comes in at the door, this is a source of complications. The intervention of love is a difficulty, for love, though blind, is unfortunately not dumb, and habitually uses speech for the concealment of truth. It does this with the best of intentions, and the best of intentions generally yield the worst of results. It should be said that sheer intellect is very seldom displayed by man. Intellect is the ideal skeleton of a man's mental power. It may be defined as an aspiration toward material advantage, absolute truth, or achievement, combined with a capacity for taking steps toward successful achievement or attaining truth. From this point of view such men as Napoleon, Machiavelli, Epictetus, Leo XIII, Bismarck, Voltaire, Anatole France, are typical intellectuals. They are not perfect: all, so far as we can tell, are tainted with moral feeling or emotion,--a frailty which probably explains why there has never been a British or American intellectual of the first rank. Huxley, Spencer, Darwin, Cromwell, all alike suffered grievously from good intentions. The British and American mind has long been honeycombed with moral impulse, at any rate since the Reformation; it is very much what the German mind was up to the middle of the nineteenth century. Intellect, as I conceive it, is seeing life sanely and seeing it whole, without much pity, without love; seeing life as separate from man, whose pains and delights are only phenomena; seeing love as a reaction to certain stimuli.

In this sense it can probably be said that no woman has ever been an intellectual. A few may have pretensions, as, for instance, "Vernon Lee," Mrs. Sidney Webb, Mrs. Wharton, perhaps Mrs. Hetty Green. I do not know, for these women can be judged only by their works. The greatest women in history--Catherine of Russia, Joan of Arc, Sappho, Queen Elizabeth--appear to have been swayed largely by their passions, physical or religious. I do not suppose that this will always be the case. For reasons which I shall indicate further on in this chapter, I believe that woman's intellect will tend toward approximation with that of man. But meanwhile it would be futile not to recognize that there exist to-day between man and woman some sharp intellectual divergences.

One of the sharpest lies in woman's logical faculty. This may be due to her education (which is seldom mathematical or scientific); it may proceed from a habit of mind; it may be the result of a secular withdrawal from responsibilities other than domestic. Whatever the cause, it must be acknowledged that, with certain trained exceptions, woman has not of logic the same conception as man. I have devoted particular care to this issue, and have collected a number of cases where the feminine conception of logic clashes with that of man. Here are a few transcribed from my notebook:

Case 33

My remark: "Most people practice a religion because they are too cowardly to face the idea of annihilation."

Case 33: "I don't see that they are any more cowardly than you. It doesn't matter whether you have a faith or not, it will be all the same in the end."

The reader will observe that Case 33 evades the original proposition; in her reply she ignores the set question, namely why people practice a religion.

Case 17

Votes for Women, of January 22, 1915, prints a parallel, presumably drawn by a woman, between two police-court cases. In the first a man, charged with having struck his wife, is discharged because his wife intercedes for him. In the second a woman, charged with theft, is sent to prison in spite of her husband's plea. The writer appears to think that these cases are parallel; the difference of treatment of the two offenders offends her logic. From a masculine point of view two points differentiate the cases:

In the first case the person who may be sent to prison is the bread-winner; in the second case it is the housekeeper, which is inconvenient but less serious.

In the first case the person who intercedes, the wife, is the one who has suffered; in the second case the person who intercedes, the husband, has not suffered injury. The person who has suffered injury is the one who lost the goods.

Case 51

This case is peculiar as it consists in frequent confusion of words. The woman here instanced referred to a very ugly man as looking Semitic. She was corrected and asked whether she did not mean simian, that is, like a monkey. She said, "Yes," but that Semitic meant looking like a monkey. When confronted with the dictionary, she was compelled to acknowledge that the two words were not the same, but persisted in calling the man Semitic, and seriously explained this by asserting that Jews look like monkeys.

Case 51, in another conversation, referred to a man who had left the Church of England for the Church of Rome as a "pervert." She was asked whether she did not mean "convert."

She said, "No, because to become a Roman Catholic is the act of a pervert."

As I thought that this might come from religious animus, I asked whether a Roman Catholic who entered a Protestant church was also a pervert.

Case 51 replied, "Yes."

Case 51 therefore assumes that any change from an original state is abnormal. The application to the charge of bad logic consists in this further test:

I asked Case 51 whether a man originally brought up in Conservative views would be a pervert if he became a Liberal.

Case 51 replied, "No."

On another occasion Case 51 referred to exaggerated praise showered upon a popular hero, and said that the newspapers were "belittling" him.

I pointed out that they were doing the very contrary; that indeed they were exaggerating his prowess.

Confronted with the dictionary, and the meaning of "belittle", which is "to cheapen with intent", she insisted that "belittling" was the correct word because "the result of this exaggerated praise was to make the man smaller in her own mind."[1]

[1] The notes as to Case 51 have not an absolute bearing upon logic in general, but the reasons put forth in her defense by Case 51 are indicative of a certain kind of logic which is not masculine. I must add that Case 51 is a woman of very good education, with many general interests.--THE AUTHOR.

Case 63

In the course of a discussion on the war in which Case 63 has given vent to moral and religious views, she remarks, "Thou shalt not kill."

I: "Then do you accept war?"

Case 63: "War ought to be done away with."

I (attempting to get a straight answer): "Do you accept war?"

Case 63: "One must defend one's self."

Upon this follows a long argument in which I attempt to prove to Case 63 that one defends, not one's self but the nation. When in difficulties she repeats, "One must defend one's self."

She refuses to face the fact that if nobody offered any resistance, nobody would be killed; she completely confuses the defense of self against a burglar with that of a nation against an invader. Finally she assumes that the defense of one's country is legitimate, and yet insists on maintaining with the Bible that one may not kill!

Case 33

Case 33: "Why didn't America interfere with regard to German atrocities in Belgium?"

I: "Why should she?"

Case 33: "America did protest when her trade was menaced."

I: "Yes. America wanted to protect her interests, but does it follow that she should protest against atrocities which do not menace her interests?"

Case 33: "But her interests are menaced. Look at the trade complications; they've all come out of that."

Case 33 has confused trade interests with moral duty; she has confused two issues: atrocities against neutrals and destruction of American property. When I tell her this, she states that there is a connection: that if America had protested against atrocities, the war would have proceeded on better lines because the Germans would have been frightened.

I: "How would this have affected the trade question?"

Case 33 does not explain but draws me into a morass of moral indignation because America protested against trade interference and not against atrocities. She finally says America had no right to do the one without the other, which logically is chaos. She also demands to be told what was the use of America's signing the Geneva Convention and the Hague Convention. She ignores the fact that these conventions do not bind anybody to fight in their defense but merely to observe their provisions. I would add that Case 33 is a well-educated woman, independent in views, and with a bias toward social questions.

Naturally, where there is a question of love, feminine logic reaches the zenith of topsy-turvy-dom. Here is a dialogue which took place in my presence.

Case 8

Case 8, who was about to be married, attacked a man who had had a pronounced flirtation with her because he suddenly announced that he was engaged.

Case 8: "How can you be so mean?"

The man: "But I don't understand. You're going to be married. What objection can you have to my getting engaged?"

Case 8: "It's quite different." Nothing could move Case 8 from that point of view.[2]

[2] Probably owing to woman's having for centuries been taught to regard the vain aspirations of the male as her perquisites.--THE AUTHOR.

I do not contend that bad logic is the monopoly of woman, for man is also disposed to believe what he chooses in matters such as politics, wars, and so forth, and then to try to prove it. Englishmen as well as Englishwomen find victory in the capture of a German trench, insignificance in the loss of a British trench; man, as well as woman, is quite capable of saying that it always rains when the Republicans are in power, should he happen to be a Democrat; man also is capable of tracing to a dinner with twelve guests the breaking of a leg, while forgetting the scores of occasions on which he dined in a restaurant with twelve other people and suffered no harm. Man is capable of every unreasonable deduction, but he is more inclined to justify himself by close reasoning. In matters of argument, man is like the Italian brigand who robs the friar, then confesses and asks him for absolution; woman is the burglar unrepentant. This may be due to woman as a rule having few guiding principles or intellectual criteria. She often holds so many moral principles that intellectual argument with her irritates the crisper male mind. But she finds it difficult to retain a grasp upon a central idea, to clear away the side issues which obscure it. She can seldom carry an idea to its logical conclusion, passing from term to term; somewhere there is a solution of continuity. For this reason arguments with women, which have begun with the latest musical play, easily pass on, from its alleged artistic merit, to its costumes, their scantiness, their undesirable scantiness, the need for inspection, inspectors of theaters, and, little by little, other inspectors, until one gets to mining inspectors and possibly to mining in general. The reader will observe that these ideas are fairly well linked. All that happens is that the woman, tiring of the central argument, has pursued each side issue as it offered itself. This comes from a lack of concentration which indisposes a woman to penetrate deeply into a subject; she is not used to concentration, she does not like it. It might lead her to disagreeable discoveries.

It is for this reason--because she needs to defend purely emotional positions against man, who uses intellectual weapons--that woman is so much more easily than man attracted by new religions and new philosophies--by Christian Science, by Higher Thought, by Theosophy, by Eucken, by Bergson. Those religions are no longer spiritual; they have an intellectual basis; they are not ideal religions like Christianity and Mohammedanism and the like, which frankly ask you to make an act of faith; what they do is to attempt to seduce the alleged soul through the intellect. That is exactly what the aspiring woman demands: emotional satisfaction and intellectual concession. Particularly in America, one discovers her intellectual fog in the continual use of such words as mental, elemental, cosmic, universality, social harmony, essential cosmos, and other similar ornaments of the modern logomachy.

Case 16

Case 16 told me that my mind did not "functionalize" properly. And gave me as an authority for the statement Aristotle, before whom, of course, I bow.

A singular and suggestive fact is that woman generally displays pitiless logic when she is dealing with things that she knows well. An expert housekeeper is the type, and there are no lapses in her argument with a tradesman. It is a platitude to mention the business capacity of the Frenchwoman, and many women are expert in the investment of money, in the administration of detail, in hospital management, in the rotation of servants' holidays (which, in large households, is most complex). It would appear that woman is unconcentrated and inconsequent only where she has not been properly educated, and this has a profound bearing on her future development. There is a growing class, of which Mrs. Fawcett, Mrs. Havelock Ellis, the Countess of Warwick, Miss Jane Addams, are typical, who have bent their minds upon intellectual problems; women like Miss Emma Goldman; like Miss Mary McArthur, whose grasp of industrial questions is as good as any man's. They differ profoundly from the average feminine literary artist, who is almost invariably unable to write of anything except love. I can think of only one modern exception,-- Miss Amber Reeves; among her seniors, Mrs. Humphry Ward is the most notable exception, but not quite notable enough.

This tendency is, I believe, entirely due to woman having always been divorced from business and politics, to her having been until recently encouraged to delight in small material possessions, while discouraged from focusing on anything non-material except religion, and from considering general ideas. Particularly as regards general ideas woman has lived in a bad atmosphere. The French king who said to his queen, "Madam, we have taken you to give us children and not to give us advice," was blowing a chill breath upon the tender shoot of woman's intelligence. Neither he nor other men wished women to conceive general ideas: women became incapable of conceiving or understanding them. Thence sprang generalization, the tendency in woman to make sweeping statements, such as "All men are deceivers," or "Men can do what they like in the world," or "Men cannot feel as women do." It is not that they dislike general questions, but that they have been thrust back from general questions, so that they cannot hold them. Here is a case:

Case 2

With the object of entertaining an elderly lady, who is an invalid, I explain, in response to her own request, the case that Germany makes for having declared war. She asks one or two questions, and then suddenly interrupts me to ask what I have been doing with myself lately in the evenings.

This is a case of interest in the particular as opposed to the general. It is an instance of what I want to show,--that woman drifts toward the particular because she has been driven away from the general. To concentrate too long upon the general is to her merely fatiguing. Doubtless because of this, many middle-aged women become exceedingly dull to men. So long as they are young all is well, for few men care what folly issues from rosy lips. But once the lips are no longer rosy, then man fails to find the companion he needs, because companionship, as differentiated from love, can rest only on mental sympathy. Middle-aged man is often dull too; while the middle-aged woman may concern herself overmuch with the indigestion of her pet dog, the middle-aged man is often unduly moved by his own indigestion. But, broadly speaking, a greater percentage of middle-aged and elderly men than of such women are interested in political and philosophical questions.

These men are often dull for another reason: they are more conventional. The reader may differ from me, but I believe that woman is much less conventional than man. She does all the conventional things and attacks other women savagely for breaches of convention. But you will generally find that where a man may with impunity break a convention he will not do so, while, if secrecy is guaranteed, a woman will please herself first and repent only if necessary. It follows that a man is conventional because he respects convention; woman conventional because she is afraid of what may happen if she does not obey convention. I submit that this shows a greater degree of conventionality in man. The typical Englishman of the world, wrecked on a desert island, would get into his evening clothes as long as his shirts lasted; I do not think his wife, alone in such circumstances, would wear a low-cut dress to take her meal of cocoanuts, even if her frock did up in front.

It is this unconventionality that precipitates woman into the so-called new movements in art or philosophy. She reacts against what is, seeking a new freedom; even if she is only seeking a new excitement, a new color, a new god, unconsciously she seeks a more liberal atmosphere, while man is nearly always contented with the atmosphere that is. When he rebels, his tendency is to destroy the old sanctuary, hers to build a new sanctuary. That is a form of idealism,--not a very high idealism, for woman seldom strains toward the impossible. In literature I cannot call to mind that woman has ever conceived a Utopia such as those imagined by Bellamy, Samuel Butler, William Morris, and H. G. Wells. The only woman who voiced ideas of this kind was Mary Wollstonecraft, and her views were hardly utopian. Nothings, such as Utopias, have been always too airy for woman. The heroes in the novels she has written, until recently and with one or two exceptions,--such as some of the heroes of George Eliot,--are either stagey or sweet. Mr. Rochester is stagey, Grandcourt is stagey, while the hero of "Under Two Flags" is merely Turkish Delight.

3

A quality which singularly contrasts with woman's vague idealism is the accuracy she displays in business. This is due to her being fundamentally inaccurate. It is not the accurate people who are always accurate; it is the inaccurate people on their guard.[3] Woman's interest in the particular predisposes her to the exact, for accuracy may be defined as a continuous interest in the particular. I suspect that it indicates a probability that by education, and especially encouragement, woman may develop a far higher degree of concentration than she has hitherto done. In her way stands a fatal facility, that of grasping ideas before they are half-expressed. It is a quality of imagination, natural rather than induced. Any schoolteacher will confirm the statement that in a mixed class, aged eleven to twelve, the essays of the girls are better than those of the boys. This is not so in a mixed university. I suspect that this latter is quite as much due to the academic judgment, which does not recognize imagination, as to the fact that in the later years of their lives the energies of girls are diverted from intellectual concentration (and also expression) toward the artistic and the social. This untrained concentration produces a certain superficiality and an impetuousness which harmonize with the intrusion of side issues,--to which I have referred,--and with the burgeoning of side issues on the general idea.

[3] I have observed for two years the steady growth in the accuracy of the work of Case 33, due to her having concentrated upon her instinctive inaccuracy.--THE AUTHOR.

Nowhere is this better shown than in the postscript habit. Men do not, as a rule, use postscripts, and it is significant that artists and persons inclined toward the arts are much more given to postscripts than other kinds of men. One might almost say that women correspond by postscript; some of them put the subject of the letter in the postscript, as the scorpion keeps his poison in his tail. I have before me letters from Case 58, with two postscripts, and one extraordinary letter from Case 11, with four postscripts and a sentence written outside the envelope. This is the apogee of superficiality. The writers have run on, seduced by irrelevance, and have not been able to stop to consider in all its bearings the subject of the letter. Each postscript represents a development or qualification, which must indicate the waste by bad education of what may be a very good mind.

I would say in passing that we should not attach undue importance to woman's physical disabilities. It is true that woman is more conscious of her body than is man. So long as he is fed, sufficiently busy, in good general health, he is normal. But woman is far more often in an unbalanced physical condition. There is a great deal to be said for the Hindu philosophical point of view, that the body needs to be just so satisfied as to become imperceptible to the consciousness, as opposed to the point of view of the Christian ascetics, who unfortunately carried their ideas so far that they ended by thinking more of their hair shirt than of Him for whose sake they wore it. In this sense woman is intellectually handicapped because her body obtrudes itself upon her. It is a subject of brooding and agitation. I suspect that this is largely remediable, for I am not convinced that it is woman's peculiar physical conditions that occasionally warp her intellect; it is equally possible that a warped intellect produces unsatisfactory physical conditions. Therefore, if, as I firmly believe that we can, we develop this intellect, profound changes may with time appear in these physical conditions.

4

The further qualification of woman's intellect is in her moral attitude. I would ask the reader to divest himself of the idea that "moral" refers only to matters of sex. Morality is the rule of conduct of each human being in his relations with other human beings, and this covers all relations. Because in some senses the morality of woman is not the morality of man, we are not entitled to say with Pope that

"Woman's at best a contradiction still."

She is a contradiction. Man is a contradiction, apparently of a different kind, and that is all. Thence spring misunderstandings and sometimes dislike, as between people of different nations. I do not want to labor the point, but I would suggest that in a very minor degree the apparent difference between man and woman may be paralleled by the apparent difference between the Italian and the Swede, who, within two generations, produce very similar American children. But man, who generalizes quite as wildly as woman when he does not understand, is determined to emphasize the difference in every relation of life. For instance, it is commonly said that woman cannot keep her promise. This seems to me entirely untrue; given that as a rule woman's intellect is not sufficiently educated to enable her to find a good reason for breaking her promise, it is much more difficult for her to do so. For we are all moral creatures, and if a man must steal the crown jewels, he is happier if he can discover a high motive for so doing. Man has a definite advantage where a loophole has to be found, and I have known few women capable of standing up in argument against a trained lawyer who has acquired the usual dexterity in misrepresentation.

In love and marriage, particularly, woman will keep plighted troth more closely than man; there is no male equivalent of jilt, but the male does jilt on peculiar lines; while a woman who knows that her youth, her beauty are going must bring things to a head by jilting, the male is never in a hurry, for his attractions wane so very slowly. Why should he jilt the woman,--make a stir? So he just goes on. In due course she tires and releases him, when he goes to another woman. That is jilting by inches, and as regards faithfulness a pledged woman is more difficult to win away than a pledged man. (To be just, it should be said that unfaithfulness is in the eyes of most men a small matter, in the eyes of most women a serious matter.) A pledged woman will remain faithful long after love has flown; the promise is a mystic bond; none but a tall flame can hide the ashes of the dead love. And so, when Shakespeare asserts,--

"Frailty, thy name is woman,"

he is delivering one of the hasty judgments that abound in his solemn romanticism.

This applies in realms divorced from love,--in questions of money, such as debts or bets. Women do run up milliners' bills, but men boast of never paying their tailors. And if sometimes women do not discharge the lost bet, it is largely because a tradition of protection and patronage has laid down that women need not pay their bets. Besides, women usually pay their losses, while several men have not yet discharged their debts of honor to me. It is a matter of honesty, and I think the criminal returns for the United States would produce the same evidence as those for England and Wales. In 1913 there were tried at Assizes for offences against property 1616 men and 122 women. The records of Quarter Sessions and of the courts of Summary Jurisdiction yield the same result, an enormous majority of male offenders,-- though there be more women than men in England and Wales! And yet, in the face of such official figures, of the evidence of every employer, man cherishes a belief in woman's dishonesty! One reason, no doubt, is that woman's emotional nature leads her, when she is criminal, to criminality of an aggravated kind. She then justifies Pope's misogynist lines:

"O woman, woman! When to ill thy mind Is bent, all hell contains no fouler fiend."

Most men, however, have abandoned the case against woman's dishonesty and confine themselves to describing her as a liar, forgetting that they generally dislike the truth when it comes from a woman's lips, and always when it reflects upon their own conduct. For centuries man has asked that woman should flatter, but also that she should tell the truth: such a confusion of demands leads the impartial mind to the conclusion that vanity cannot be a monopoly of the female. But it is quite true that woman does not always cherish truth so well as man. The desire for truth is intellectual, not emotional. Truth is a cold bed-fellow, as might be expected of one who rose from a well. And among women cases of disinterested lying are not uncommon. Here is Case 16:

An elderly woman talked at length about not having received insurance papers, and made a great disturbance. It later appeared that she had not insured. On another occasion she informed the household that her son-in-law had been cabled to from South Africa to come and visit his dying mother. It was proved that no cable had been sent.

I have a number of cases of this kind, but this is the most curious. I suspect that this sort of lying is traceable to a need for romance and drama in a colorless life. It springs from the wish to create a romantic atmosphere round one's self and to increase one's personal importance. Because men hold out hands less greedy toward drama and romance they are less afflicted, but they do not entirely escape, and we have all observed the new importance of the man whose brother has been photographed in a newspaper or, better still, killed in a railway accident. If he has been burned in a theater, the grief of his male relatives is subtly tinged with excited delight. Romance, the wage of lies, is woman's compensation for a dull life.

5

Vanity is as old as the mammoth. Romantic lying, obviously connected with vanity, is justly alleged to be developed in woman. No doubt woman's chief desire has been to appear beautiful, and it is quite open to question whether the leaves that clothed our earliest ancestress were gathered in a spirit of modesty rather than in response to a desire for adornment.

But it should not be too readily assumed that vanity is purely a feminine characteristic. It is a human characteristic, and the favor of any male savage can be bought at the price of a necklace of beads or of an admiral's cocked hat. The modern man is modish too, as much as he dares. At Newport as at Brighton the dandy is supreme. It would be inaccurate, however, to limit vanity to clothes. Vanity is more subtle, and I would ask the reader which of the three principal motives that animate man--love, ambition, and gold lust-- is the strongest. The desire to shine in the eyes of one's fellows has produced much in art and political service; it has produced much that is foolish and ignoble. It has led to political competition, to a wild race for ill-remunerated offices, governorships, memberships of Parliament. Representatives of the people often wish to serve the people; they also like to be marked out as the people's men. There are no limits to masculine desire for honors; seldom in England does a man refuse a peerage; Frenchmen are martyrs to their love of ribbons, and not a year passes without a scandal because an official has been bribed to obtain the d'Honneur for somebody, or, funnier still, because an adventurer has blacked his face, set up in a small flat, impersonated a negro potentate, and distributed for value received grand crosses of fantastic kingdoms. Even democratic Americans have been known to seek titled husbands for their daughters, and a few have become Papal barons or counts.

Male vanity differs from female, but both are vanity. The two sexes even share that curious form of vanity which in man consists in his calling himself a "plain man", bragging of having come to New York without shoes and with a dime in his pocket; which, in woman, consists in neglecting her appearance. Both sexes convey more or less: "I am what I am, a humble person ... but quite good enough." The arrogance of humility is simply repulsive.

Ideas such as the foregoing may proceed from a certain simplicity. Woman is much less complex than the poets believe. For instance, many men hold that woman's lack of self-consciousness, as exemplified by disturbances in shops, has its roots in some intricate reasoning process. One must not be carried away: the truth is that woman, having so long been dependent upon man, has an exaggerated idea of the importance of small sums. Man has earned money; woman has been taught only to save it. Thus she has been poor, and poverty has caused her to shrink from expenditure; often she has become mean and, paradoxically enough, she has at the same time become extravagant. Poverty has taught her to respect the penny, while it has taught her nothing about the pound. If woman finds it quite easy to spend one tenth of the household income on dress, and even more,[4] it is because her education makes it as difficult for her to conceive a thousand dollars as it is for a man to conceive a million. It is merely a question of familiarity with money.

[4] See "Uniforms for Women," and observe extreme figures and details of feminine expenditure on clothes.

Besides, foolish economy and reckless expenditure are indications of an elementary quality. In that sense woman is still something of a savage. She is still less civilized than man, largely because she has not been educated. This may be a very good thing, and it certainly is an agreeable one from the masculine point of view. Whether we consider woman's attitude to the law, to social service, or to war, it is the same thing. In most cases she is lawless; she will obey the law because she is afraid of it, but she will not respect it. For her it is always sic volo, sic jubeo. I suspect that if she had had a share in making the law she would not have been like this, for she would have become aware of the relation between law and life. Roughly she tends to look upon the law as tyrannous if she does not like it, as protective if she does like it. Probably there is little relation between her own moral impulse, which is generous, and the law, which is only just. (That is, just in intention.) This is qualified by the moral spirit in woman, which increasingly leads her to the view that certain things should be done and others not be done. But even then it is likely that at heart woman does not respect the law; she may respect what it represents,--strength,--but not what it implies,--equity. She is infinitely more rebellious than man, and where she has power she inflames the world in protest. I do not refer to the militant suffragists, but to woman's general attitude. For instance, when it is proposed to compel women to insure their servants, to pay employer's compensation for accident, to restrict married women's control of their property, to establish laws regulating the social evil, we find female opposition very violent. I do not mean material opposition, although that does occur, but mental hostility. Woman surrenders because she must, man because he ought to.

That is an attitude of barbarism. It is a changing attitude; the ranks of social service have, during the last half-century, been disproportionately swollen by woman. Our most active worker in the causes of factory inspection, child protection, anti-sweating, is to-day woman. Woman is emerging swiftly from the barbarous state in which she was long maintained. She will change yet more,--and further on in this chapter I will attempt to show how,--but to-day it must be granted that there runs in her veins much vigorous barbarian blood. Her attitude to war is significant. During the past months I have met many women who were inflamed by the idea of blood; so long as they were not losing relatives or friends themselves, they tended to look upon the war as the most exciting serial they had ever read. Heat and heroism, what could be more romantic? Every woman to whom I told this said it was untrue, but in no country have the women's unions struck against war; the suffragettes have organized, not only hospitals, but kitchens, recreation rooms, canteens for the use of soldiers; many have clamored to be allowed to make shells; some, especially in Russia, have carried rifles. In England, thirteen thousand women volunteered to make war material; women filled the German factories. Of course, I recognize that this is partly economic: women must live in wartime even at the price of men's lives, and I am aware that a great many women have done all they could to arrest the spread of war. In England many have prevented their men from volunteering; in America, I am told, women have been solid against war with Germany. But let the reader not be deceived. A subtle point arises which is often ignored. If women went to war instead of men, their attitude might be different. Consider, indeed, these two paragraphs, fictitious descriptions of a battlefield:--

"Before the trenches lay heaped hundreds of young men, with torn bodies, their faces pale in the moonlight. The rays lit up the face of one that lay near, made a glitter upon his little golden moustache."

"Before the trenches lay heaped hundreds of young girls. The moonlight streamed upon their torn bodies and their fair skins. The rays fell upon one that lay near, drawing a glow from the masses of her golden hair."

Let the masculine reader honestly read these two paragraphs (which I do not put forward as literature). The first will pain him; the second will hurt him more. That men should be slaughtered--how hateful! That girls should be slaughtered--it is unbearable. Here, I submit, is part of woman's opposition to war, of the exaggerated idea people have of her humanitarian attitude. I will not press the point that as a savage she may like blood better than man; I will confine myself to suggesting that a large portion of her opposition to war comes out of a sexual consciousness; it seems horrible to her that young men should be killed, just as horrible as my paragraph on the dead girls may seem to the male reader.

Some men have seen women as barbarous and dangerous only, have based their attitude upon the words of Thomas Otway: "She betrayed the Capitol, lost Mark Antony to the world, laid old Troy in ashes." This is absurd; if man cannot resist the temptation of woman, he can surely claim no greater nobility. Mark Antony "lost" Cleopatra by wretched suicide as much as she "lost" him. If because of Helen old Troy was laid in ashes, at least another woman, guiltless Andromache, paid the price. To represent woman so, to suggest that there were only two people in Eden, Adam and the Serpent, is as ridiculous as making a woman into a goddess. It is the hope of the future that woman shall be realized as neither diabolical nor divine, but as merely human.

6

We must recognize that the emotional quality in woman is not a characteristic of sex; it is merely the exaggeration of a human characteristic. For instance, it is currently said that women make trouble on committees. They do; I have sat with women on committees and will do it again as seldom as possible: their frequent inability to understand an obvious syllogism, their passion for side issues, their generalizations, and their particularism whenever emotion is aroused, make committee work very difficult. But every committee has its male member who cannot escape from his egotism or from his own conversation. What woman does man does, only he does it less. The difference is one of degree, not of quality.

Where the emotionalism of women grows more pronounced is in matters of religion and love. There is a vague correspondence between her attitude to the one and to the other, in outwardly Christian countries, I mean. She often finds in religion a curious philter, both a sedative and a stimulant. Religion is often for women an allotrope of romance; blind as an earthworm she seeks the stars, and it is curious that religion should make so powerful an appeal to woman, considering how she has been treated by the faiths. The Moslem faith has made of her a toy and a reward; the Jewish, a submissive beast of burden; the Christian, a danger, a vessel of impurity. I mean the actual faiths, not their original theory; one must take a faith as one finds it, not as it is supposed to be, and in the case of woman the Christian religion is but little in accord with the view of Him who forgave the woman taken in adultery. The Christian religion has done everything it could to heap ignominy upon woman: head-coverings in church, practical tolerance of male infidelity, kingly repudiation of queens, compulsory child-bearing, and a multiplicity of other injustices. The Proverbs and the Bible in general are filled with strictures on "a brawling woman", "a contentious woman"; when man is referred to, mankind is really implied. Yet woman has kissed the religious rods. One might think that indeed she was seduced and held only by cruelty and contempt. She is now, in a measure, turning against the faiths, but still she clings to them more closely than man because she is more capable of making an act of faith, of believing that which she knows to be impossible.

The appeal of religion to woman is the appeal of self-surrender,--that is, ostensibly. In the case of love it is the same appeal, ostensibly; though I suspect that intuition has told many a woman who gave herself to a lover or to a god that she was absorbing more than she gave: in love using the man for nature whom she represents, in faith performing a pantheistic prodigy, the enclosing of Nirvana within her own bosom.

But speculation as to the impulse of sex in relation to religion, in Greece, in Egypt, in Latin countries, would draw me too far. I can record only that to all appearances a portion of the religious instinct of woman is derived from the love instinct, which many believe to be woman's first and only motive. It is significant that among the sixty-five cases upon which this article is based there are several deeply religious single women, while not one of the married women shows signs of more than conventional devotion. I incline to believe that woman is firstly animal, secondly, intellectual; while man appears to be occasionally animal and primarily intellectual.

Observe indeed the varying age at which paternal and maternal instincts manifest themselves. A woman's passion for her child generally awakes at birth, and there are many cases where an unfortunate girl, intending to murder her child, as soon as it is born discovers that she loves it. On the other hand, a great many men are indifferent to their children in infancy and are drawn to them only as they develop intellectual quality. This is just the time when woman drifts from them. Qualified by civilized custom, the attitude of woman toward her child is very much that of the cat toward her kitten; as soon as the kitten is a few weeks old, the mother neglects it. A few months later she will not know it. Her part is played. So it is not uncommon to find a woman who has been enthralled by her baby giving it over entirely to hired help: the baby is growing intellectualized; it needs her no more except as a kindly but calm critic. And frequently at that time the father begins to intervene, to control the education, to prepare for the future. Whether in the mental field this means much more than the difference in temperament between red hair and black hair (if that means anything), I do not know; but it is singular that so often the mother should drift away from her child just at the moment when the father thinks of teaching it to ride and shoot and tell the truth. Possibly by that time her critical work is done.

Indicative of the influence of the emotions is the peculiar intensification of love in moments of crisis, such as war, revolution, or accident. Men do not escape this any more than women: the German atrocities, for instance, largely proceed from extreme excitement. But men have but slender bonds to break, being nearly all ready to take their pleasure where they can, while women are more fastidious. Woman needs a more highly charged atmosphere, the whips of fear or grief, the intoxication of glory. When these are given her, her emotions more readily break down her reserves; and it is not remarkable that in times of war there should be an increase in illegitimate births as well as an increase in marriages. Woman's intellect under those pressures gives way. A number of the marriages contracted by British soldiers about to leave for the front are simple manifestations of hysteria.

As for caprice, it has long been regarded as woman's privilege, part of her charm. Man was the hunter, and his prey must run. Only he is annoyed when it runs too fast. He is ever asking woman to charm him by elusiveness and then complaining because she eludes him. There is hardly a man who would not to-day echo Sir Walter Scott's familiar lines,--

"O Woman! in our hours of ease Uncertain, coy, and hard to please, And variable as the shade By the light quivering aspen made."

It is not woman's fault. The poetry of the world is filled with the words "to win" and "to woo"; one cannot win or woo one who does not baffle; one can only take her, and men are not satisfied to do only that. Man loves sincerity until he finds it; he can live neither with it nor without it; this is true most notably in the lists of love. He is for falsehood, for affectation, lest the prize should too easily be won. Both sexes are equally guilty, if guilt there be.

More true is it that many women lie and curvet as a policy because they believe thus best to manage men. They generally believe that they can manage men. They look upon them as "poor dears." They honestly believe that the "poor dears" cannot cook, or run houses, or trim hats, ignoring the fact that the "poor dears" do these things better than anybody, in kitchens, in hotels, and in hat shops. Especially they believe that they can outwit them in the game of love. This curious idea is due to woman's consciousness of having been sought after in the past and told that she did not seek man but was sought by him. Centuries of thraldom and centuries of flattery have caused her to believe this--the poor dear!

In ordinary times, when no world-movements stimulate, the chief exasperation of woman resides in jealousy. It differs from male jealousy, for the male is generally possessive, the female competitive. I suspect that Euripides was generalizing rashly when he said that woman is woman's natural ally. She is too sex-conscious for that, and many of us have observed the annoyance of a mother when her son weds. Competition is always violent, so much so that woman is generally mocking or angry if a man praises ever so slightly another woman. If she is young and able to make a claim on all men, she tends to be still more virulent because her claim is on all men. This is partly due to the marriage market and its restrictions, but it is also partly natural. No doubt because it is natural, woman attempts to conceal that jealousy, nature being generally considered ignoble by the civilized world. In this respect we must accept that an assumption of coldness is considered a means of enticing man. It may well be that, where woman does not exhibit jealousy, she is with masterly skill suggesting to the man a problem: why is she not jealous? On which follows the desire to make her jealous, and entanglement.

Because of these powerful preoccupations, when woman adopts a career she has hitherto frequently allowed herself to be diverted therefrom by love. Up to the end of the nineteenth century it was very common for a woman to abandon the stage, the concert platform, and so forth, when she married. A change has come about, and there is a growing tendency in women, whether or not at the expense of love I do not know, to retain their occupations when they marry. But the tendency of woman still is to revert to the instinctive function. In days to come, when we have developed the individual and broken up the socialized society in which we live, when the home has been swept away and the family destroyed, I do not believe that this factor will operate so powerfully. In the way of change stand the remnants of woman's slavish habit. No longer a slave, she tends to follow, to submit, to adjust her conduct to the wish of man, and it is significant that a powerful man is seldom henpecked. The henpecked deserve to be henpecked, and I would point out that there is no intention in these notes to attempt to substitute henpecked husbands for cockpecked wives. The tendency is all the other way, for woman tends to mould herself to man.

A number of cases lie before me:

Case 61 married a barrister. Before her marriage she lived in a commercial atmosphere; after marriage she grew violently legal in her conversation. Her husband developed a passion for motoring; so did Case 61. Observe that during a previous attachment to a doctor, Case 61 had manifested a growing interest in medicine.

Case 18 comes from a hunting family, married a literary man, and within a few years has ceased to take any exercise and mixes exclusively with literary people.

Case 38, on becoming engaged to a member of the Indian Civil Service, became a sedulous student of Indian literature and religion. On her husband's appointment to a European post, her interest did not diminish. She has paid a lengthy visit to India.

There are compensating cases among men: I have two. In one case a soldier who married a literary woman has turned into a scholar. In the other a commercial man, who married a popular actress, has been completely absorbed by the theater, and is now writing successful plays.

It would appear from these rather disjointed notes that the emotional quality in woman is more or less at war with her intellectual aims. Indeed it is sometimes suggested that where woman appears, narrowness follows; that books by women are mostly confined to love, are not cosmic in feeling. This is generally true, for reasons which I hope to indicate a little farther on; but it is not true that books where women are the chief characters are narrow. Such novels as Anna Karenina, Madame Bovary, Une Vie, Tess of the D'Urbervilles make that point obvious. As a rule, books about men, touching as they do, not only upon love, but upon art, politics, business, are more powerful than books about women. But one should not forget that books written round women are mostly written by women. As women are far less powerful in literature than men, we must not conclude that books about women are naturally lesser than books about men. The greatest books about women have been written by men. But few men are sufficiently unprejudiced to grasp women; only a genius can do so, and that is why few books about women exist that deserve the epithet great. It remains to be seen whether an increased understanding of the affairs of the world will develop among women a literary power which, together with the world, will embrace herself.

7

In the attempt to indicate what the future may reserve for woman, it is important to consider what she has done, because she has achieved much in the face of conservatism, of male egotism, of male jealousy, of poverty, of ignorance, and of prejudice. These chains are weaker to-day, and the goodwill that shall not die will break them yet; but many women, a few of whose names follow, gave while enslaved an idea of woman's quality.

Examine indeed this short list:[5]

[5] I associate the arts with intellectual quality. (See "Woman and the Paintpot.") Broadly, I believe that all achievements, artistic or otherwise, proceed from intellect.

Painting: Angelica Kauffmann, Madame Vig 閑 le Brun, Rosa Bonheur.

Music and drama: Rachel, Siddons, Ellen Terry, Sarah Bernhardt, Teresa Carre 駉, Sadayacco.

Literature: George Eliot, Jane Austen, the Bronte, Madame de Sta 雎, Madame de S 関 ign? Christina Rossetti, Elizabeth Browning. More recent, Mrs. Alice Meynell, Miss May Sinclair, "Lucas Malet," Mrs. Edith Wharton, "Vernon Lee."

Social service and politics: Mrs. Charlotte Perkins Gilman, Miss Jane Addams, Madame Montessori, Mrs. Fawcett, Mrs. Ennis Richmond, Mrs. Beecher Stowe, Florence Nightingale, Mrs. Havelock Ellis, Mrs. Sidney Webb, Miss Clementina Black, Josephine Butler, Mrs. Pankhurst, Elizabeth Fry. Observe the curious case of Mrs. Hetty Green, financier.

This list could be enormously increased, and, as it is, it is a random list, omitting women of distinction and including women of lesser distinction. But still it contains no unknown names, and, though I do not pretend that it compares with a similar list of men, it is an indication. I am anxious that the reader should not think that I want to compare Angelica Kauffmann with Leonardo, or Jane Austen with Shakespeare. In every walk of life since history began there have been a score of men of talent for every woman of talent, and there has never been a female genius. That should not impress us: genius is an accident; it may be a disease. It may be that mankind has produced only two or three geniuses, and that one or two women in days to come may redress the balance, and it may be that several women have been mute inglorious Miltons. We do not know. But in the matter of talent, notably in the arts, I submit that woman can be hopeful, particularly because most of the names I give are those of women of the nineteenth century. The nineteenth century was better for woman than the eighteenth, the eighteenth better than the seventeenth: what could be more significant? In the arts I feel that woman has never had her opportunity. She has been hailed as an executive artist, actress, singer, pianist; but as a creator, novelist, poet, painter, she has been steadfastly discounted,--told that what she did was very pretty, until she grew unable to do anything but the pretty-pretty. She has grown up in an atmosphere of patronage and roses, deferential, subservient. She has persistently been told that certain subjects were "not fit for nice young ladies"; she has been shut away from the expression of life.

Here is a typical masculine attitude, that of Mr. George Moore, in A Modern Lover. Mr. George Moore, who seems to know a great deal about females but less about women, causes in this book Harding, the novelist, who generally expresses him, to criticize George Sand, George Eliot, and Rosa Bonheur: "If they have created anything new, how is it that their art is exactly like our own? I defy any one to say that George Eliot's novels are a woman's writing, or that The Horse Fair was not painted by a man. I defy you to show me a trace of feminality in anything they ever did; that is the point I raise. I say that women as yet have not been able to transfuse into art a trace of their sex; in other words, unable to assume a point of view of their own, they have adopted ours."

This is cool! I have read a great deal of Mr. George Moore's art criticism: when it deals with the work of a man he never seeks the masculine touch. He judges a man's work as art; he will not judge a woman's work as art. He starts from the assumption that man's art is art, while woman's art is--well, woman's art. That is the sort of thing which has discouraged woman; that is the atmosphere of tolerance and good-conduct prizes which she has breathed, and that is the stifling stupidity through which she is breaking. She will break through, for I believe that she loves the arts better than does man. She is better ground for the development of a great artist, for she approaches art with sympathy, while the great bulk of men approach it with fear and dislike, shrinking from the idea that it may disturb their self-complacency. The prejudice goes so far that, while women are attracted to artists as lovers, men are generally afraid of women who practice the arts, or they dislike them. It is not a question of sex; it is a question of art. All that is part of sexual heredity, of which I must say a few words.

But, before doing so, let me waste a few lines on the male conception of love, which has influenced woman because love is still her chief business. To this day, though it dies slowly, the male attitude is still the attitude to a toy. It is the attitude of Nietzsche when saying, "Man is for war, woman for the recreation of the warrior." This idea is so prevalent that Great Britain, in its alleged struggle against Nietzschean ideas, is making abundant use of the Nietzschean point of view. No wonder, for the idea runs not only through men but through Englishmen: "woman is the reward of war,"--that is a prevalent idea, notably among men who make war in the neighborhood of waste-paper baskets. It has been exemplified by the British war propaganda in every newspaper and in every music hall, begging women to refuse to be seen with a man unless he is in khaki. It has had government recognition in the shape of recruiting posters, asking women "whether their best boy is in khaki." It has been popularly formulated on picture postcards touchingly inscribed, "No gun, no girl."

All that--woman as the prize (a theory repudiated in the case of Belgian atrocities)--is an idea deeply rooted in man. In the eighteen-sixties the customary proposal was, "Will you be mine?" Very faintly signs are showing that men will yet say, "May I be yours?" It will take time, for the possessive, the dominating instinct in man, is still strong; and long may it live, for that is the vigor of the race. Only we do not want that instinct to carry man away, any more than we want a well-bred horse to clench its teeth upon the bit and bolt.

We want to do everything we can to get rid of what may be called the creed of the man of the world, which is suggested as repulsively as anywhere in Mr. Rudyard Kipling's Departmental Ditties:

"My Son, if a maiden deny thee and scufflingly bid thee give o'er, Yet lip meets with lip at the lastward--get out! She has been there before. They are pecked on the ear and the chin and the nose who are lacking in lore.

"Pleasant the snaffle of Courtship, improving the manners and carriage; But the colt who is wise will abstain from the terrible thornbit of Marriage. Blister we not for bursati? So when the heart is vext, The pain of one maiden's refusal is drowned in the pain of the next."

There is a great deal of this sort of thing in Moliere, in Thackeray, in Casanova. The old idea of woman eluding and lying; of woman stigmatized if she has "been there before", while man may brag of having "been there before" as often as possible; of man lovelacing for his credit's sake and woman adventuring at her peril.

8

I submit that each man and woman has two heredities: one the ordinary heredity from two parents and their forbears, the other more complex and purely mental--the tradition of sex. Heredity through sex may be defined as the resultant of consecutive environments. I mean that a woman, for instance, is considerably influenced by the ideas and attitudes of her mother, grandmothers, and all female ascendants. They had a tradition, and it is the basis of her outlook. Any boy born in a slum can, as he grows educated, realize that the world lies before him; literature and history soon show him that many as lowly as he have risen to fame, as artists, scientists, statesmen; he may even dream of becoming a king, like Bonaparte. To the boy nothing is impossible; if he is brave, there is nothing he may not tear from the world. He knows it, and it strengthens him; it gives him confidence. What his fathers did, he may do; the male sexual heredity is a proud heritage, and only yesterday a man said to me, "Thank God, I am a man." Contrast with this the corresponding type of heredity in woman. Woman carries in her the slave tradition of her maternal forbears, of people who never did anything because they were never allowed to; who were told that they could do nothing but please, until they at last believed it, until by believing they lost the power of action; who were never taught, and because uneducated were ashamed; who were never helped to understand the work of the world, political, financial, scientific, and, therefore, grew to believe that such realms were not for them. I need not labor the comparison: obviously any woman, inspired by centuries of dependence, instinctively feels that, while everything is open to man, very little is open to her. She comes into the arena with a leaden sword; in most cases she hardly has energy to struggle.

A little while ago, when Britain was floating a large war loan, one woman told me that she could not understand its terms. We went into them together, and she found that she understood perfectly. She was surprised. She had always assumed that she did not understand finance, and the assumption had kept her down, prevented her from understanding it. Likewise, and until they try, many women think they cannot read maps and time-tables.

With that heredity environment has coalesced, and I think no one will deny that a continuous suggestion of helplessness and mental inferiority must affect woman. It means most during youth, when one is easily snubbed, when one looks up to one's elders. By the time one has found out one's elders, it is generally too late; the imprint is made, and woman, looking upon herself as inferior, hands on to her daughters the old slavery that was in her forbears' blood. To me this seems foolish, and during the past thirty or forty years a great many have come to think so too; they have shown it by opening wide to woman the doors of colleges, many occupations and professions. Many are to-day impatient because woman has not done enough, has not justified this new freedom. I think they are unjust; they do not understand that a generation of training and of relative liberty is not enough to undo evils neolithic in origin. All that we are doing to-day by opening gates to women is to counter-influence the old tradition, to implant in the woman of to-morrow the new faith that nothing is beyond her powers. It lies with the woman of to-day to make that faith so strong as to move mountains. I think she will succeed, for I doubt whether any mental power is inherent in sex. There are differences of degree, differences of quality; but I suspect that they are mainly due to sexual heredity, to environment, to suggestion, and that indeed, if I may trench upon biology, human creatures are never entirely male or entirely female; there are no men, there are no women, but only sexual majorities.

The evolution of woman toward mental assimilation with man, though particularly swift in the past half-century, has been steady since the Renaissance. Roughly, one might say that the woman of the year 1450 had no education at all; in this she was more like man than she ever was later, for the knights could not read, and learning existed only among the priests. The time had not yet come for the learned nobleman; Sir Philip Sidney, the Earl of Surrey, the Euphuists, had not yet dispelled the medieval fogs, and few among the laymen, save Cheke and Ascham, had any learning at all. In those days woman sang songs and brought up babies. Two hundred and fifty years later the well-to-do woman had become somebody; she could even read, though she mainly read tales such as The Miraculous Love of Prince Alzamore. She was growing significant in the backstairs of politics. Sometimes she took a bath. Round about 1850 she turned into the "perfect lady" who kept an album bound in morocco leather. She wrote verses that embodied yearnings.

Often she had a Turkish parlor, and usually as many babies as she could. But already the Bronte and George Eliot had come to knock at the door; Miss Braddon was promising to be, if not a glory, at least a power, and before twenty years were out, John Stuart Mill was to lead the first suffragettes to the House of Commons.

To-day it is another picture: woman in every trade except those in which she intends to be; woman demanding and using political power; woman governing her own property; woman senior to man in the civil service. She has not yet her charter, and still suffers much from the tradition of inferiority, from her lack of confidence in herself. But many women are all ambition, and within the last year two young women novelists have convinced me that the thing they most desire is to be great in their art. Whether they will succeed does not matter much; what does matter is that they should harbor such a wish. Whether woman's physical disabilities, her present bias toward unduly moral and inadequately intellectual judgments, will forever hamper her, I do not know; but I do not think so. Whether the influence of woman, more inherently lawless, more anarchic than man, will result in the breaking down of conventions and the despising of the law, I do not know either. But if the world is to be remoulded, I think it much more likely to be remoulded by woman than by man, simply because that as a sex he is in power, and the people who are in power never want to alter anything.

Woman's rebellion is everywhere indicated: her brilliance, her failings, her unreasonableness, all these are excellent signs of her revolt. She is even revolting against her own beauty; often she neglects her clothes, her hair, her complexion, her teeth. This is a pity, but it must not be taken too seriously: men on active service grow beards, and woman in her emancipation campaign is still too busy to think of the art of charming. I suspect that as time passes and she suffers less intolerably from a sense of injustice, she will revert to the old graces. The art of charming was a response to convention; and of late years unconventionality, a great deal of which is ridiculous, has grown much more among women than among men. That is not wonderful, for there were so many things woman might not do. Almost any movement would bring her up against a barrier; that is why it seems that she does nothing in the world except break barriers. How genuine woman's rebellion is, no man can say. It may be that woman's impulse toward male occupations and rights is only a reaction against the growing difficulty of gaining a mate, children, and a home. But I very much more believe that woman is straining toward a new order, that the swift evolution of her mind is leading her to contest more and more violently the assumption that there are ineradicable differences between the male and the female mind. As she grows more capable of grasping at education, she will become more worthy of it; her intellect will harden, tend to resemble that of man; and so, having escaped from the emptiness of the past into the special fields which have been conceded her, she will make for broader fields, fields so vast that they will embrace the world.

II

FEMINIST INTENTIONS

1

The Feminist propaganda--which should not be confounded with the Suffrage agitation--rests upon a revolutionary biological principle. Substantially, the Feminists argue that there are no men and that there are no women; there are only sexual majorities. To put the matter less obscurely, the Feminists base themselves on Weininger's theory, according to which the male principle may be found in woman, and the female principle in man. It follows that they recognize no masculine or feminine "spheres", and that they propose to identify absolutely the conditions of the sexes.

Now there are two kinds of people who labor under illusions as regards the Feminist movement, its opponents and its supporters: both sides tend to limit the area of its influence; in few cases does either realize the movement as revolutionary. The methods are to have revolutionary results, are destined to be revolutionary; as a convinced but cautious Feminist, I do not think it honest or advisable to conceal this fact. I have myself been charged by a very well-known English author (whose name I may not give, as the charge was contained in a private letter) with having "let the cat out of the bag" in my little book, Woman and To-morrow. Well, I do not think it right that the cat should be kept in the bag. Feminists should not want to triumph by fraud. As promoters of a sex war, they should not hesitate to declare it, and I have little sympathy with the pretenses of those who contend that one may alter everything while leaving everything unaltered.

An essential difference between "Feminism" and "Suffragism" is that the Suffrage is but part of the greater propaganda; while Suffragism desires to remove an inequality, Feminism purports to alter radically the mental attitudes of men and women. The sexes are to be induced to recognize each other's status, and to bring this recognition to such a point that equality will not even be challenged. Thus Feminists are interested rather in ideas than in facts; if, for instance, they wish to make accessible to women the profession of barrister, it is not because they wish women to practice as barristers, but because they want men to view without surprise the fact that women may be barristers. And they have no use for knightliness and chivalry.

Therein lies the mental revolution: while the Suffragists are content to attain immediate ends, the Feminists are aiming at ultimate ends. They contend that it is unhealthy for the race that man should not recognize woman as his equal; that this makes him intolerant, brutal, selfish, and sentimentally insincere. They believe likewise that the race suffers because women do not look upon men as their peers; that this makes them servile, untruthful, deceitful, narrow, and in every sense inferior. More particularly concerned with women, it is naturally upon them and their problems that they are bringing their first attention to bear.

The word "inferior" at once arouses comment, for here the Feminist often distinguishes himself from the Suffragist. He frequently accepts woman's present inferiority, but he believes this inferiority to be transient, not permanent. He considers that by removing the handicaps imposed upon women, they will be able to win an adequate proportion of races. His case against the treatment of women covers every form of human relation: the arts, the home, the trades, and marriage. In every one of these directions he proposes to make revolutionary changes.

The question of the arts need not long detain us. It is perfectly clear that woman has had in the past neither the necessary artistic training, nor the necessary atmosphere of encouragement; that families have been reluctant to spend money on their daughter's music, her painting, her literary education, with the lavishness demanded of them by their son's professional or business career. Feminists believe that when men and women have been leveled, this state of things will cease to prevail.

In the trades, English Feminists resent the fact that women are excluded from the law, generally speaking, the ministry, the higher ranks of business and of the Civil Service and so forth, and practically from hospital appointments; also that women are paid low wages for work similar to that of men.

They complain too that the home demands of woman too great an expenditure of energy, too much time, too much labor; that the concentration of her mind upon the continual purchasing and cooking of food, on cleaning, on the care of the child, is unnecessarily developed; they doubt if the home can be maintained as it is if woman is to develop as a free personality.

With marriage, lastly, they are perhaps most concerned. Though they are not in the main prepared to advocate free union, they are emphatically arrayed against modern marriage, which they look upon as slave union. The somewhat ridiculous modifications of the marriage service introduced by a few couples in America and by one in England, in which the word "obey" was deleted from the bride's pledge, can be taken as indicative of the Feminist attitude. Their grievances against the home, against the treatment of women in the trades, are closely connected with the marriage question, for they believe that the desire of man to have a housekeeper, of woman to have a protector, deeply influence the complexion of unions which they would base exclusively upon love, and it follows that they do not accept as effective marriage any union where the attitudes of love do not exist. For them who favor absolute equality, partnership, sharing of responsibilities and privileges, modern marriage represents a condition of sex-slavery into which woman is frequently compelled to enter because she needs to live, and in which she must often remain, however abominable the conditions under which the union is maintained, because man, master of the purse, is master of the woman.

Generally, then, the Feminists are in opposition to most of the world institutions. For them the universe is based upon the subjection of woman: subjection by law, and subjection by convention. Before considering what modifications the Feminists wish to introduce into the social system, a few words must be said as to this distinction between convention and the law.

Convention, which is nothing but petrified habit, has lain upon woman perhaps more heavily than any law, for the law can be eluded with comparative ease, and she who eludes it may very well become a heroine, merely because we are mostly anarchists and dislike the law. Every man is in himself a minority, and is opposed to the law because the law is the expression of the will of the majority, that is to say, the will of the vulgar, of the norm. But convention is far more subtle: it is the result of the common agreement of wills. Therefore, as it is a product of unanimity, the penalties which follow on the infractions of its behests are terrible; she who infringes it becomes, not a heroine, but an outcast. The law is, then, nothing by the side of etiquette.

Hence Feminist propaganda. While the Suffragists wish to alter the law, the Feminists wish to alter also the conventions. It may not be too much to say that they would almost be content with existing laws if they could change the point of view of man, make him take for granted that women may smoke, or ride astride, or fight; cease to be surprised because Madame Dieulafoy chooses to wear trousers; briefly, renounce the subjective fetich of sex. Still, as they realize that states become more socialistic every day, they realize also that through the law only can they hope to change manners. The mental revolution which they intend to effect must therefore be prefaced by a legal revolution.

The first Feminist intention is economic,--proceeds on two lines:

1. They intend to open every occupation to women.

2. They intend to level the wages of women and men.

As regards the first point, they are not as a rule unreasonable. If they demand that women should practice the law as they do in France, preach the Gospel as they do in the United States of America, bear arms, as in Dahomey, it is not because they attach any great value to these occupations, but because they consider that any limitation put upon woman's activities is intrinsically degrading; so keenly do they feel this, that some serious

Feminists took part some years ago in the controversy on, "Are there female angels?"

The second point is more important. It is a well-established fact that women are paid less than men for the same work: for instance, in England, women begin at wages which are less than those of men as teachers, post-office and other civil servants. The Feminists are not prepared to agree that this condition is due to some inherent inferiority of woman: in their view her inferiority is transitory, is due to her inferior position. One Feminist, C. Gascoigne Hartley, in The Truth About Women, outlines a bold hypothesis: "What, then, is the real cause of the lowness of remuneration offered to women for work when compared with men? Thousands of women and girls receive wages that are insufficient to support life. They do not die, they live; but how? The answer is plain. Woman possesses a marketable value attached to her personality which man has not got. The woman's sex is a saleable thing." Briefly, if a woman works less well than a man, less fast, less continuously, it is because she is inadequately rewarded. They reverse the common position that woman is not well paid because woman is not competent, basing themselves on the parallel that liberty alone fits men for liberty. They argue that woman is not competent because she is not well paid; consequently, those Feminists who are inclined toward Radicalism in politics demand a minimum wage in all trades, which shall be the same for women and men.

The economic change will be brought about by revolutionary methods, by sex strikes and sex wars. The gaining of the vote is, in the Feminist's view, nothing but an affair of outposts. Conscious propagandists do not intend to allow the female vote to be split as it might recently have been between Mr. Roosevelt, Mr. Wilson, and Mr. Taft. They intend to use the vote to make women vote as women, and not as citizens; that is to say, they propose to sell the female vote en bloc to the party that bids highest for it in the economic field. To the party that will, as a preliminary, pledge itself to level male and female wages in government employ, will be given the Feminist vote; and if no party will bid, then it is the Feminist intention to run special candidates for all offices, to split the male parties, and to involve them in consecutive disasters such as the one which befell the Republican party in the last presidential election in the United States.

Side by side with this purely political action, Feminists intend to use industrial strikes in exactly the same manner as do the Syndicalist railwaymen, miners, and postmen of Europe; well aware that they have captured a number of trades, such as millinery, domestic service, restaurant attendance, and so forth, and large portions of other trades, such as cotton-spinning in Lancashire, they propose to use as a basis the vote and the political education that follows thereon, to induce women to group themselves in women's trade-unions, by means of which they will hold up trades, and when they are strong enough, hold up society itself.

I enunciate these views with full sympathy, which can hardly be refused when one realizes that the sweated trades are almost entirely in the hands of women,--laundry, box-making, toys, artificial flowers, and the like. The fact that the underpaid trades are women's trades, and that the British Government has been compelled to institute wage-boards to bring up women's pay from four cents an hour to the imposing figure of six cents, and the recent white-slavery investigations in America, are evidence enough that public opinion should hesitate before blaming any industrial steps women may choose to take. For it should not be forgotten that woman risks more than comfort and health, and that the underpayment of her sex often forces her to degradation.

Conscious of the temporary inferiority of woman, an inferiority traceable to centuries of neglect and belittling patronage, the Feminists propose to increase woman's power by making her fitter for power. They are well aware that the enormous majority of women receive but an inferior education, that in their own homes, especially in the South of England, they are not encouraged to read the newspaper (which I believe to be a more powerful instrument of intellectual development than the average serious book), and that any attempt on their part to acquire more information, to attend lectures, to join debating clubs, tends to lower their "charm value" in the eyes of men. That point of view they are determined to alter in the male. They propose to kill the prejudice by the homoeopathic method: that is to say, to educate woman more because man thinks she is already too educated. Briefly, to kill poison by more poison. For this purpose they intend to throw open education of all grades to women as well as to men, to remove such differences as exist in England, where a woman cannot obtain an Oxford or Cambridge degree. They propose to raise the school age of both sexes, and to not less than sixteen. The object of this, so far as women are concerned, is to prevent the exploitation of little girls of fourteen, notably as domestic servants.

Some Feminists favor co-education, on the plea that it enables the sexes to understand each other, and these build principally on the success of American schools. A more violent section, however, desires to place the education of girls entirely in the hands of women, partly because they wish to enhance the sex war, and partly because they consider that continual intercourse between the sexes tends to deprive ultimate love of its mystery and its charm. But both sections fully agree that the broadest possible education must be given to every woman, so as to fit her for contest with every man.

3

So much, then, for the mental revolution and its eventual effects on the position of women in the arts, the trades, and the schools. In the industrial section, especially, we have already had an indication of the main line of the Feminist attitude, a claim to a right to choose. This right is indeed the only one for which the Feminists are struggling, and they struggle for those obscure reasons which lie at the root of our wish to live and to perpetuate the race. It is no wonder, then, that the Feminists should have designs upon the most fundamental of human institutions, marriage and motherhood.

In the main, Feminists are opposed to indissoluble Christian marriage. Some satisfaction has been given to them in a great many states by the extension of divorce facilities, but they are not content with piecemeal reform such as has been carried out in the United States, for they realize quite well that divorce cuts both ways, and that it is not satisfactory for a wife to be married in one state, and divorced under a slack law in another. Indeed I believe that one of the first Feminist demands in America would be for a federal marriage law.

But alterations in the law are minor points by the side of the emotional revolution that is to be engineered. Roughly speaking, we have to-day reasonable men and instinctive women. Such notably was Ibsen's view: "Woman cannot escape her primitive emotions." But he thought she should control these inevitables so far as possible: "As soon as woman no longer dominates her passions, she fails to achieve her objects."[6] The distinction between reason and instinct, however, is not so wide as it seems; for reason is merely the conscious use of observation, while instinct is the unconscious use of the same faculty; but as the trend of Feminism is to make woman self-conscious and sex-conscious, the Feminists can be said broadly to be warring against instinct, and on the side of reason. They look upon instinct as indicative of a low mentality. For instance, the horse is less instinctive than the zebra, and a curious instance of this was yielded by certain horses in the South African war, which were unable to crop the grass because they had always eaten from mangers. Civilization, we may say, had caused the horses to degenerate, but nobody will contend that the horse is not more intelligent than the zebra, more capable of love, even of thought. Briefly, the horse approximates more closely to a reasonable being than does the instinctive wild beast.

[6] La Femme dans le Th 殳 tre d'Ibsen, by FRIEDERICKE BOETTCHER.--THE AUTHOR.

The Feminists therefore propose, by training woman's reason, to place her beyond the scope of mere emotion and mere prejudice, to enable her to judge, to select a mate for herself and a father for her children,--a double and necessary process.

There is a flavor of eugenics about these ideas: the right to choose means that women wish to be placed in such a position that, being economically independent to the extent of having equal opportunities, they will not be compelled to sell themselves in marriage as they now very often do. I do not refer to entirely loveless marriages, for these are not very common in Anglo-Saxon states, but to marriages dictated by the desire of woman to escape the authority of her parents, and to gain the dignity of a wife, the possession of a home and of money to spend. In the Feminist view, these are bad unions because love does not play the major part in them, and often plays hardly any part at all. The Feminists believe that the educated woman, informed on the subject of sex-relations, able to earn her own living, to maintain a political argument, will not fall an easy prey to the offer held out to her by a man who will be her master, because he will have bought her on a truck system.

Under Feminist rule, women will be able to select, because they will be able to sweep out of their minds the monetary consideration; therefore they will love better, and unless they love, they will not marry at all. It is therefore probable that they will raise the standard of masculine attractiveness by demanding physical and mental beauty in those whom they choose; that they will apply personal eugenics. The men whom they do not choose will find themselves in exactly the same position as the old maids of modern times: that is to say, these men, if they are unwed, will be unwed because they have chosen to remain so, or because they were not sought in marriage. The eugenic characteristic appears, in that women will no longer consent to accept as husbands the old, the vicious, the unpleasant. They will tend to choose the finest of the species, and those likely to improve the race. As the Feminist revolution implies a social revolution, notably "proper work for proper pay", it follows that marriage will be easy, and that those women who wish to mate will not be compelled to wait indefinitely for the consummation of their loves. Incidentally, also, the Feminists point out that their proposals hold forth to men a far greater chance of happiness than they have had hitherto, for they will be sure that the women who select them do so because they love them, and not because they need to be supported.

This does not mean that Feminism is entirely a creed of reason; indeed a number of militant Feminists who collected round the English paper, The Freewoman, have as an article of their faith that one of the chief natural needs of woman and society is not less passion, but more. If they wish to raise women's wages, to give them security, education, opportunity, it is because they want to place them beyond material temptations, to make them independent of a protector, so that nothing may stand in the way of the passionate development of their faculties. To this effect, of course, they propose to introduce profound changes in the conception of marriage itself.

Without committing themselves to free union, the Feminists wish to loosen the marriage tie, and they might not be averse to making marriage less easy, to raising, for instance, the marriage age for both sexes; but as they are well aware that, in the present state of human passions, impediments to marriage would lead merely to an increase in irregular alliances, they lay no stress upon that point. Moreover, as they are not prepared to admit that any moral damage ensues when woman contracts more than one alliance in the course of her life,--which view is accepted very largely in the United States, and in all countries with regard to widows,--they incline rather to repair the effects of bad marriages, than to prevent their occurrence.

Plainly speaking, the Feminists desire simpler divorce. They are to a certain extent ready to surround divorce with safeguards, so as to prevent the young from rushing into matrimony; indeed they might "steep up" the law of the "Divorce States." On the other hand, they would introduce new causes for divorce where they do not already exist, and they would make them the same for women and men. For instance, in Great Britain a divorce can be granted to a man on account of the infidelity of his wife, while it can be granted to a woman only if to infidelity the husband adds cruelty or desertion. Such a difference the Feminists would sweep away, and they would probably add to the existing causes certain others, such as infectious and incurable diseases, chronic drunkenness, insanity, habitual cruelty, and lengthy desertion. It should be observed that the campaign is thus as favorable to men as it is to women, for many men who have now no relief would gain it under the new laws. As Feminism is international, the programme of course includes the introduction of divorce where it does not exist,--in Austria, Spain, South American states, and so forth.

What exact form the new divorce laws would take, I cannot at present say, for Feminism is as evolutionary as it is revolutionary, and Feminists are prepared to accept transitory measures of reform. Thus, in the existing circumstances, they would accept a partial extension of divorce facilities, subject to an adequate provision for all children. In the ultimate condition, to which I refer later on, this might not be necessary, but as a temporary expedient, Feminists desire to protect woman while she is developing from the chattel condition to the free-woman condition. Until she is fit for her new liberty, it is necessary that she should be enabled to use this liberty without paying too heavy a price therefor. Indeed this clash between the transitory and the ultimate is one of the difficulties of Feminism. The rebels must accept situations such as the financial responsibility of man, while they struggle to make woman financially independent of man, and it is for this reason that different proposals appear in the works of Ellen Key, Rosa Mayreder, Charlotte Gilman, Olive Schreiner, and others, but these divergences need not trouble us, for Feminism is an inspiration rather than a gospel, and if it lays down a programme, it is a temporary programme.

Personally, I am inclined to believe that the ultimate aim of Feminism with regard to marriage is the practical suppression of marriage and the institution of free alliance. It may be that thus only can woman develop her own personality, but society itself must so greatly alter, do so very much more than equalize wages and provide work for all, that these ultimate ends seem very distant. They lie beyond the decease of Capitalism itself, for they imply a change in the nature of the human being which is not impossible when we consider that man has changed a great deal since the Stone Age, but is still inconceivably radical.

Ultimate ends of Feminism will be attained only when socialization shall have been so complete that the human being will no longer require the law, but will be able to obey some obscure but noble categorical imperative; when men and women can associate voluntarily, without thrall of the State, for the production and enjoyment of the goods of life. How this will be achieved, by what propaganda, by what struggles and by what battles, is difficult to say; but in common with many Feminists I incline to place a good deal of reliance on the ennobling of the nature of the male. That there is a sex war, and will be a sex war, I do not deny, but the entry of women into the modern world of art and business shows that an immense enlightenment has come over the male, that he no longer wishes to crush as much as he did, and therefore that he is loving better and more sanely. Therein lies a profound lesson: if men do not make war upon women, women will not make war upon men. I have spoken of sex war, but it takes two sides to make a war, and I do not see that in the event of conflict the Feminists can alone be guilty.

One feature manifests itself, and that is a change of attitude in woman with regard to the child. Indications in modern novels and modern conversation are not wanting to show that a type of woman is arising who believes in a new kind of matriarchate, that is to say, in a state of society where man will not figure in the life of woman except as the father of her child. Two cases have come to my knowledge where English women have been prepared to contract alliances with men with whom they did not intend to pass their lives,--this because they desired a child. They consider that the child is the expression of the feminine personality, while after the child's birth, the husband becomes a mere excrescence. They believe that the "Wife" should die in childbirth, and the "Mother" rise from her ashes. There is nothing utopian about this point of view, if we agree that Feminists can so rearrange society as to provide every woman with an independent living; and I do not say that this is the prevalent view. It is merely one view, and I do not believe it will be carried to the extreme, for the association of human beings in couples appears to respond to some deep need; still, it should be taken into account as an indication of sex revolt.

That part of the programme belongs to the ultimates. Among the transitory ideas, that is, the ideas which are to fit Feminism into the modern State, are the endowment of motherhood and the lien on wages. The Feminists do not commit themselves to a view on the broad social question whether it is desirable to encourage or discourage births. Taking births as they happen, they lay down that a woman being incapacitated from work for a period of weeks or months while she is giving birth to a child, her liberty can be secured only if the fact of the birth gives her a call upon the State. Failing this, she must have a male protector in whose favor she must abdicate her rights because he is her protector. As man is not handicapped in his work by becoming a father, they propose to remove the disability that lies upon woman by supplying her with the means of livelihood for a period surrounding the birth, of not less than six weeks, which some place at three months. There is nothing wild in this scheme, for the British Insurance Act (1912) gives a maternity endowment of seven dollars and fifty cents whether a mother be married or single. The justice of the proposal may be doubted by some, but I do not think its expediency will be questioned. On mere grounds of humanity, it is barbarous to compel a woman to labor while she is with child; on social grounds it is not advantageous for the race to allow her to do so: premature births, child-murder, child-neglect by working mothers, all these facts point to the social value of the endowment.

4

The last of the transitory measures is the lien on wages. In the present state of things, women who work in the home depend for money on husbands or fathers. The fact of having to ask is, in the Feminists' view, a degradation. They suggest that the housekeeper should be entitled to a proportion of the man's income or salary, and one of them, Mrs. M. H. Wood, picturesquely illustrates her case by saying that she hopes to do away with "pocket-searching" while the man is asleep. Mrs. Wood's ideas certainly deserve sympathy; though many men pay their wives a great deal more than they are worth and are shamefully exploited--a common modern position--it is also quite true that many others expect their wives to run their household on inadequate allowances, and to come to them for clothes or pleasure in a manner which establishes the man as a pasha. When women have grown economically independent, no lien on wages will be required, but meanwhile it is interesting to observe that there has recently been formed in England a society called "The Home-makers' Trade Union", one of whose specific objects is, "To insist as a right on a proper proportion of men's earnings being paid to wives for the support of the home."

Generally speaking, then, it is clear that women are greatly concerned with the race, for all these demands--support of the mother, support of the child, rights of the household--are definitely directed toward the benevolent control by the woman of her home and her child. I have alluded above to these Feminist intentions: they affect the immediate conditions as well as the ultimate.

Among the ultimates is a logical consequence of the right of woman to be represented by women. So long as Parliamentary Government endures, or any form of authority endures, the Feminists will demand a share in this authority. It has been the custom during the Suffrage campaign to pretend that women demand merely the vote. The object of this is to avoid frightening the men, and it may well be that a number of Suffragists honestly believe that they are asking for no more than the vote, while a few, who confess that they want more, add that it is not advisable to say so; they are afraid to "let the cat out of the bag", but they will not rest until all Parliaments, all Cabinets, all Boards are open to women, until the Presidential chair is as accessible to them as is the English throne. Already in Norway women have entered the National Assembly: they propose to do so everywhere. They will not hesitate to claim women's votes for women candidates until they have secured the representation which they think is their right, that is, one half.

These are the bases, roughly outlined, on which can be established a lasting peace.

I do not want to exaggerate the difficulties and perils which are bound up in this revolutionary movement, but it is abundantly clear that it presupposes profound changes in the nature of women and of men. While man will be asked for more liberalism and be expected to develop his sense of justice (which has too long lain at the mercy of his erratic and sentimental generosity), woman will have to modify her outlook. She is now too often vain, untruthful, disloyal, avaricious, vampiric; briefly she has the characteristics of the slave. She will have to slough off these characteristics while she is becoming free, she will have to justify by her mental ascent the increase in her power. Feminists are not blind to this, and that is why they lay such stress upon education and propaganda.

One of the most profound changes will, I think, appear in sex relations. The "New Woman", as we know her to-day, a woman who is not so new as the woman who will be born of her, is a very unpleasant product; armed with a little knowledge, she tends to be dogmatic in her views and offensive in argument. She tends to hate men, and to look upon Feminism as a revenge; she adopts mannish ways, tends to shout, to contradict, to flout principles because they are principles; also she affects a contempt for marriage which is the natural result of her hatred of man. The New Woman has not the support of the saner Feminists. Says Ellen Key, in The Woman Movement, "These cerebral, amaternal women must obviously be accorded the freedom of finding the domestic life, with its limited but intensive exercise of power, meagre beside the feeling of power which they enjoy as public personalities, as consummate women of the world, as talented professionals. But they have not the right to falsify life values in their own favor so that they themselves shall represent the highest form of life, the 'human personality', in comparison with which the 'instinctive feminine' signifies a lower stage of development, a poorer type of life." If this were the ultimate type, very few men would be found in the Feminist camp, for the coming of the New Woman would mean the death of love. If the death of love had to be the price of woman's emancipation, I, for one, would support the institution of the zenana and the repression of woman by brute force; but I do not think we need be anxious.

If the New Woman is so aggressive, it is because she must be aggressive if she is to win her battle. We cannot expect people who are laboring under a sense of intolerable injury to set politely about the righting of that injury: when woman has entered her kingdom she will no longer have to resort to political nagging; her true nature will affirm itself for the first time, for it is difficult to believe that it has been able to affirm itself under the entirely artificial conditions of androcracy. Already some women to whom a profession or mental eminence has given exceptional freedom show us in society that women can be free and yet be sweet. Indeed they almost demonstrate the Feminist contention that women must be free before they are sweet, for are not these women--of whom all of us can name a few--the noblest and most desirable of their kind? The New Woman is like a freshly painted railing: whoever touches it will stain his hands, but the railing will dry in time.

There is one type of woman, however, whom I venture to call "Old Woman", who is probably a bitterer foe of Feminism than any man, and that is the super-feminine type, the woman for whom nothing exists except her sex, who has no interests except the decking of her body and the quest of men. This woman, who once dominated her own species, still represents the majority of her sex. It is still true that the majority of women are concerned with little save the fashions, novels, plays, and vaudeville turns. These women want to have "a good time" and want nothing more; they are ready to prey upon men by flattering them; they encourage their own weakness, which they call "charm", and generally aim at being pampered slaves, because, from their point of view, it pays better than being working partners. Evidence of this is to be found in women's shops, in the continual change in fashions, each of which is a signal to the male, and in the continual increase in the sums spent on adornment: it is not uncommon for a rich woman to spend five hundred dollars on a frock; two hundred and fifty dollars has been given for a hat; and twenty-five thousand dollars for a set of furs.

As Miss Beatrice Tina very well says, "Woman is woman's worst enemy", though she is not referring to this type. So long as woman maintains this attitude, compels men to forget her soul in the contemplation of her body, so long will she remain a slave, for this preoccupation goes further than clothes.

In a book recently published,[7] an account is given of the late Empress of Austria, who was evidently one of the lowest of the slave type. It is noteworthy that she had no love for her children because their coming had impaired her beauty. Now I do not suggest that Feminists are arrayed against the care of the body; far from it, for the campaign has many associates among those who support physical culture, the fresh-air movement, ancient costume revival, and the like; but Feminists are well aware that concentration on adornment diverts woman from the development of her brain and her soul, and enhances in her the characteristics of the harem favorite. One tentative suggestion is being made, and that is a uniform for women. The interested parties point out that men practically wear uniform, that there is hardly any change from year to year in their costume, and that any undue adornment of the male is looked upon as bad form. Thus, while few men can with impunity spend more than five hundred dollars a year on their clothes, many women do not consider themselves happy unless they can dispose of anything between five and twenty times that amount. This, while involving the household in difficulties, lowers the status of woman by lowering her mentality.

[7] My Past, by COUNTESS MARIE LARISCH.

Feminists do not ask for sumptuary laws, having very little respect for the law, but for a new vision, which is this: Man, intellectually developed, decks himself in no finery, because it is not essential to his success; woman must likewise abandon frippery if she is to have energy enough to reach his plane. They propose to attain their object by the force of their example, and I have received several letters on the subject, which show that the idea of fixing the fashions is not entirely wild, for fashion consists after all in wearing what everybody wears, and if an influential movement is started to maintain the costume of women on a very simple basis, it may very well prevail and kill much of their purely imitative vanity by showing them that undue devotion to self-adornment is very much worse than immoral: in other words, that it is in bad taste.

Incidentally the Feminists believe that the downfall of many women is procured by the offer of fine clothes. They hope, therefore, to derive some side-profits from the simplification of woman's dress.

The question also arises as to whether woman can become intellectually independent, whether she does not naturally depend upon the opinion of man. It is suggested that not even rich women are actually independent, that women place marriage above their art, their work; but I do not think this is a very solid objection, for the vaunted independence of men is not so very common; they currently take many of their opinions from their reading in newspapers and books, and must often subordinate their views and their conduct to the will of their employer. The main answer to this suggestion is that we must not consider woman as she was, but woman "as she is becoming", as a creature of infinite potentialities, as virgin ground.

It may be petitio principii to say that, as woman has produced so much that is fine, she would have produced very much more if she had not been hampered by law and custom, derided by the male, but bad logic is often good sense. This should commend itself to men who are no longer willing to support the idea that women are inherently inferior to them, but who are willing to give them an opportunity to develop in every field of human activity. Thus and thus only, if man will readjust his views, expel vir and enthrone homo, can woman cease to appear before him as a rival and a foe, realize herself in her natural and predestined role, that of partner and mate.[8]

[8] Note: This chapter should be taken as the summary of an intellectual position. Its points are considered in detail in the four chapters that follow.

III

UNIFORMS FOR WOMEN

1

The change which has come over politics reflects closely enough the change which has come about in the direction of man's desire. In times of peace, diplomacy and the affairs of kings have given place to wages and the housing of the poor; that which was serious has become pompous; that which was of no account now stands in the foreground. And so it is not absurd to suggest that one of those things which once made jests for the comic paper and the Victorian paterfamilias has, little by little, with the spread of wealth, become a problem of the day, a problem profound and menacing, full of intimations of social decay, not far remote in its reactions from the spread of a disease.

That problem is the problem of women's dress, or rather it is the problem of the fashions in women's dress. Women have never been content merely to clothe themselves, nor, for the matter of that, until very recently, have men; but men have grown a new sanity, while women, if we read aright the signs of the times, have grown naught save a new insanity. We have come to a point where, for a great number of women, the fashions have become the motive power of life, and where, for almost every woman, they have acquired great importance. Women classify each other according to their clothes; they have corrupted the drama into a showroom; they have completely ruined the more expensive parts of the opera house; they have invaded the newspapers in myriad paragraphs, in fashion-pages, and do not spare even the august columns of the most dignified papers. This preoccupation does not exist among men. We have had our dandies and we still have our "nuts" and dudes; but it never served a man very well to be a dandy or a beau, and most of us to-day suspect that if the "nut" were broken, he would be found to contain no kernel.

Men have escaped the fashions and therewith they have spared themselves much loss of energy and money. For it is not only the fashions that matter: it is the cost of women's clothes, the intrinsic cost; it is their continual changes for no reason, changes which sometimes produce, and sometimes destroy, beauty; sometimes promote comfort, and often cause torture. But always by their drafts upon its wealth, women lead humanity nearer to poverty, envy, discontent, frivolity, starvation, prostitution,--to general social degradation. Nothing can mitigate these evils until woman is induced to view clothing as does the modern man, until, namely, she decides to wear a uniform.

2

The costliness of women's clothes would not be so serious if the fashions did not change at so bewildering a speed. We have come to a point where women have not time to wear out their clothes, flimsy though they be; where we ought to welcome the adulteration of silk and wool; where we ought to hope that every material may get shoddier and more worthless, so that the new model may have a chance to justify its short life by the badness of the stuff. To-day women will quite openly say, "I won't buy that. I couldn't wear it out." They actually want to wear out their clothes! The causes of this are obvious enough. We are told that there are "rings" in Paris, London, and Vienna which decree every few months that the clothes of yesterday have become a social stigma; this is true, but much truer is the view that women are in the grasp of a new hysteria; that, lacking the old occupations of brewing, baking, child-rearing, spinning, they are desperately looking for something to do. They have found it: they are undoing the social system.

It was not always so. It is true that all through history, even in biblical times, moralists and preachers inveighed against the gewgaws that woman loves. They cried out before they were hurt; if he were alive to-day, Bossuet might, for the first time, fail to find words.

To the old curse of cost we have added change, as any student of costume will confirm; for in past ages the clothing of women did not change very rapidly. There is hardly any difference between the costume of 1755 and that which Queen Marie Leszczynska wore ten years later; in Greece, between B.C. 500 and 400, the Ionic chiton and himation varied but little; the Doric chiton did not vary at all; the variations in the over-mantle were not considerable. Any examination of early sculpture, of Attic vases, or of terra cottas, will show that this is true. The ladies of Queen Elizabeth's court, together with their royal mistress, wore the same kind of clothes through their adult years. Their clothes were sometimes costly, but when bought they were bought, and until worn out were not discarded. And our grandmothers had that famous black-silk dress, so sturdy that it stood up by itself, very like a Victorian virtue; it lasted a lifetime, sometimes became an heirloom.

There was no question then of fashion following on fashion at a whirling pace. Women were clothed, sometimes beautifully, sometimes hideously, but at any rate they scrapped their gowns only when they were worn out; now they scrap them as soon as they have been worn. The results of this I deal with further on, but here already I can suggest these results by quoting a few facts. Before me lies one of Messrs. Barker's advertisements; it seems that there are reception gowns, restaurant gowns; that there are coats for the races, and coats for the car, wraps for one thing, and wraps for another--and the advertisement adds that these are the "latest novelties" for "the coming season", and that all this is "for the spring." And then there is an advertisement of Messrs. Tudor Brothers, who have gowns for Ascot, and--this is quite true--gowns for Alexandra Day.

I have looked in vain for gowns for July 23, for gowns to be worn between a quarter past eleven and half-past twelve in the morning, and for special mourning gowns for a cousin's stepfather. Some occasions are shamefully disregarded. They are not disregarded by everybody; at least I presume that the lady quoted by Mrs. Cobden-Sanderson in her lecture in March, who possessed one hundred and ten nightdresses, could cope with any eventuality; there is also the lady, mentioned to me by a friend who made some American investigations for me, who possesses one hundred and fifty pairs of slippers. There is, too, the Bon March?in Paris, where, out of a staff of six thousand to seven thousand, are employed fifteen hundred dressmakers, and where there is a special workroom for the creation of models.

As all these people must find something to do, they create, unless they merely steal from the dead; but one thing they always do, and that is destroy yesterday. Out of their activities comes a continual stream of new colors and new combinations of colors, of high heels and low heels, gilt heels and jeweled heels; they give us the spat that is to keep out the wet and then the spat that does not keep out the eye. Before me lies a picture of a spat made of lace; another of a skirt slit so high as to reveal a jeweled garter. That is creation, and I suppose I shall be told that that is art. It is art sometimes, and very beautiful, but beauty does not make it live; in fact beauty causes the creation to die more swiftly, because the more appealing it is, the more it is worn: as soon as it is worn by the many, the furious craving for distinction sweeps down upon it and slays it. There are several mad women in the St. Anne asylum in Paris whose peculiar disease is that they cannot retain the same idea for more than a few seconds; they ring the changes on a few hundreds of ideas. Properly governed, their inspirations might be valuable in Grafton Street.

I do not think the end is near; indeed, fashions will be more extreme to-morrow than they are to-day. The continual growth of wealth, and the difficulty of spending it when it clots in a few hands, will make for a greater desire to spend more, more quickly, more continually, and in wilder and wilder forms. The women are to-day having individual orgies; to-morrow will come the saturnalia.

3

There is a clear difference between the cost of women's clothes and of men's. It is absolutely impossible to dress a woman of the comfortable classes for the same amount per annum that will serve her husband well. I must quote a few figures taken from Boston, New York, and London.

Boston.--Persons considered: those having $4500 to $7500 a year.

Average price of a suit (coat and skirt), $40 ready to wear; made by a dressmaker of slight pretensions, $125 to $225.

Afternoon dresses, ready to wear, $125 to $225.

Evening dresses, absolute minimum, $50; fashionable frocks, $200 to $350.

On an income of $7500 a woman's hat will cost $25; variation, $20 to $45; hats easily attain $125.

Veils attain $5. Opera cloaks in stores, $90 to $250. Dressmakers charge $450 to $600.

New York.--Winter street dress, $225.

Skunk muff and stole, $200.

Hats for the year, at least $250 to $300.

Footwear, $250 per annum.

I am informed that a lady in active society can "manage with care" on $2500, but really needs $4500 to $5000.

A "moderate" wardrobe allows for "extremely simple" gowns costing $125 each; the lady in question requires at least six new evening dresses and six remodeled, per annum. She wore an average set of furs, price $1500.

London.--Debenham & Freebody blouse, $10.

Ponting's Leghorn hat, $8. Gorringe straws, $12 to $14.

I am informed that where the household income is $3500 to $7500 a year the ordinary prices are as follows:

Coats and skirts, $50 to $75.

Evening dresses, $75 to $120.

Hats, $7.50 to $20.

Silk stockings are cheap at $1.50, and veils at $1.50.

Now these are all moderate figures and will shock nobody, but if they are compared with the prices paid by men, they are, without any question of fashion, outrageous. I believe they are high because it is men and not women who pay, because the dressmaker trades on man's sex-enslavement. But I am concerned just now less with causes than with facts, and would rather ask how the modest $100 evening gown compares with the man's $63 dress suit (by a good tailor). How does the $63 coat and skirt compare with a man's lounge suit, price $36 by anybody save Poole, and by him only $52.50? No man has, I believe, paid more than $9 for a silk hat, while his wife pays at least $20. The point is not worth laboring, it is obvious; while every man knows that a "good cut" does not account for the discrepancy, as he too pays, but pays moderately, for the art of a good tailor. And, mark you, apart from cost, men's clothes last indefinitely, while women's, if they have the misfortune to last, must be given away.

The prices I have quoted are moderate prices, and I cannot resist the temptation to give some others which are not unusual. I am informed that $400 can easily be charged for an afternoon dress, $1000 for an evening dress, $200 for a coat and skirt; that it is quite easy to spend $5000 a year on underclothes and $250 on an aigrette. I observe a Maison Lewis Ascot hat, price $477. Yantorny will not make a shoe under $60; a pair of his shoes made of feathers is priced by him at $2400.

As for totals: I have private information of an expenditure of $30,000 a year on dress; one of $70,000 is reported to me from America. I have seen a bill for dress and lingerie alone, incurred at one shop, for $35,000 in twelve months.

4

It might be thought that this ghastly picture speaks for itself, but evidently it does not, as hardly anybody takes any notice of the question. I will venture to draw attention to the results of what is happening, ignoring the abnormal figures, because I wish to reason from what happens all the time rather than from what happens now and then, to figure the position in which the world finds itself because women do not hesitate to spend upon their clothes a full ten per cent of the household income. This figure is correct: such inquiries as I have been able to make among women of my acquaintance prove it. Out of a joint income of $12,500 a year one woman spends $1350 a year on clothes; another, out of $5750 a year, last year $655; a third, out of $8000 a year $700, but she is a "dowdy."

In households of moderate means, where a certain social status is kept up, where, for instance, a woman takes $500 a year out of $5000, while her husband dresses well on $200, when all expenses have been paid, there is money for little else; fixed charges, children, service, taxes, swallow up the rest. There is hardly anything left for books, barely for a circulating library; there is very little for the theater and for games; holidays are taken in hideous lodgings at the seaside because a comfortable bungalow costs too much. The money that should have provided the most important thing in human life, namely pleasure, is on the woman's back.

In the lower classes the case is, in a way, still worse. I do not mean workmen's wives, for any old rag will serve the slaves,--but their daughters! Recently a coroner's inquest in Soho showed that a girl had practically starved herself to death to buy fine clothes, and it is not an isolated case. For the last eight years I have been investigating the condition of workwomen, and, so far as typists, manicurists, and tea-shop girls are concerned, I assert that their main object in leaving the homes where they are kept is to have money for smart clothes; they flood the labor market at blackleg prices, to buy finery and for no other reason. They go further: while making the necessary inquiries for my novel, A Bed of Roses, I scheduled the cases of about forty London prostitutes. In about twenty-five per cent of the cases the original cause, direct or contributory, was a desire for luxury which took the form of fine clothes. Now these women tell one what they think one would like to hear, and, where they scent sympathy, as much as possible attribute their fall to man's deceit. But acumen develops in the investigator; the figure of twenty-five per cent is correct or may even be an underestimate.

The conclusion is that from fifteen thousand to twenty-five thousand women now on the streets of London have been brought there by a desire for self-adornment. Meanwhile there is no labor available for the poor consumer, because the energy of the dressmaker is diverted toward the rich; while Miss So-and-So is paid $4000 a year to design hats, the workwoman wears a man's cap rescued from the refuse heap.

I shall be told that the rich are not responsible for the luxurious desires of the poor; but that is evidently nonsense: the rich themselves are not innocent of prostitution. I have had reported the case of a well-paid Russian dancer whose dress bills are paid by two financiers; that of a French actress who calmly states that she needs three lovers, one for her hats, one for her lingerie, and one for her gowns; and a close inquiry into the "bridge losses" which occasionally provoke the fall of rich men's daughters will show that these are dressmakers' bills. All this is not without its effect upon the poor. The girl of the lower classes, hypnotized by fashion plates, compelled to witness at the doors of fashionable churches, in the street, at the music halls, and even at the picture palaces, the continuous streaming past of the fashion pageant, develops an intolerable desire for finery. You may say that she is wrong, that she should practice self-denial, but this is not an age of self-denial; luxury is in the air, we despair of happiness and take to pleasure, we feel the future life too far ahead, we want to enjoy. It is natural enough, especially for girls who are young and who feel unfairly outclassed by richer women who are neither as young nor as beautiful; but still it is base. If baseness is to go, the lesson must come from the top; if there is to be self-denial, then que messieurs les assassins commencent! Until the rich woman realizes that her example is her responsibility it will be fair to say that the Albemarle Street $500 gown has its consequence in a prostitute on the Tottenham Court Road.

The rich woman herself does not escape scot free. It is obvious that the woman chiefly occupied with thoughts of dress develops a peculiar kind of frivolity, that she becomes unfit to think of art, the public interest, perhaps of love. She is the worst social product, a parasite, and she is not even always beautiful. Sometimes she is insane: the investigations of Doctor Bernard Holz and of Doctor Rudolf Foerster connect the mania for fashion with paranoia, and have elicited extraordinary facts, such as the collection of clothes by insane women, and such as cases of pyromania which coincided with a craze for dress.

It is, indeed, quite possible that some women might go mad if they permanently felt themselves less well-dressed than their fellows; and that is the crux of the fashion idea. Woman does not desire to be beautifully dressed: she desires to be more beautifully dressed than her fellows. She wishes to insult and humiliate her sisters, and, as modern clothes are costly, she does not hesitate to give full play to human cruelty, to use all the resources of the rich husband on whom she preys to satisfy her pride and to apply her arrogant ingenuity to the torture of her sisters. And I said, "She wants to be more beautiful." Is that quite right? Partly, though what woman mainly seeks is not to be beautiful but to be fashionable; the words have become synonymous. Yet the fashions are not always beautiful; sometimes they are hideous, break every line of the body, make it awkward, hamper its movements. If women truly wanted to be beautiful they would not follow the fashions: our little dark, sloe-eyed women would dress rather like the Japanese, and our big, ox-eyed beauties would appear as Greeks; but no, Juno, Carmen, and Dante's Beatrice, all together and all in turn, don first the crinoline and then the hobble skirt.

Nor do they want to attract men. They think they do but they do not, for they know perfectly well that few men realize what they wear, that all they observe is "something blue" or an effect they call "very doggy"; they know also that men do not wed the dangerous smart, but the modest; that men fear the implication that smart women are unvirtuous, and that they certainly fear their dressmakers' bills. Nor is it even true that women want many new clothes so as to be clean: if that were true, men in their well-worn suits could not be touched with a pitchfork. The truth is that changes in fashion are a habit and a hysteria, an advertisement, an insult offered by wealth to poverty, a degradation of women's qualities which carries its own penalty in the form of growing mental baseness.

5

Well, what shall we do? Women must wear a uniform. Strictly, they already do wear a uniform, for what is a fashion but a uniform? Some years ago when musquash coats (and cheaper velveteen) were "in", and hats were very small, there were in London scores of thousands of young women so exactly alike that considerable confusion was caused at tube stations and such other places where lovers meet; this simplifies the problem of choosing the new uniform. Let it not be thought that I wish women to dress in sackcloth, though they will certainly dress in sackcloth if ever sackcloth comes in; I do not care what they wear, provided they do not continually alter its form, and provided it is not too dear. The way in which old and young, tall and short, fat and thin, force themselves into the same color and the same shape is sheer socialism; I merely want to carry the uniform idea a little further, to make it a permanent uniform.

We already have uniforms for women, apart from the fashions, uniforms which never change: those of the nurse, the nun, the parlor-maid, the tea-girl. We have national costumes, Dutch, Swiss, Irish, Japanese, Italian; we have drill suits and sports dresses. And they are not ugly. All these uniformed women have as good a chance of marriage as any others, and her ladyship gains as many proposals on the golf links as at night on the terrace. I would suggest that women should have two or three uniforms of a kind to be decided, which would never change, and, I repeat, they need not be ugly uniforms.

Men's uniforms are not ugly; I would any day exchange my lounge suit for the uniform of a guardsman--if I might wear it. In this "if" is the essence of the whole idea, the whole practicability of it. Men wear uniform, that is to say lounge suits in certain circumstances, morning coats in others, evening clothes in yet others. They never vary. We are told that they vary. Tailors show new suitings, the papers print articles about men's fashions, and perhaps a button is added or a lapel is lengthened, and that is all. Nobody cares. Men follow no fashions so far as the fable of men's fashions is true; they dare not do so, because to do so serves them ill in society. A man who dares to break through the uniform idea of his sex is generally dubbed a "bounder"; if he is one of the very young, fancy-socked, extreme-collared kind, people smile and say, "It'll wear off with time." And women, who tolerate the dandies at tea-time, love the others.

The uniform would have to be brought in by a group of leaders of fashion determined to abolish fashion. I could sketch a dozen uniforms, but women would make a great to-do, forgetting that most fashions are created by men, so I will confine myself to timid suggestions.

1. For general outdoor wear the coat and skirt is the best, together with a blouse. Lace and insertion should be abandoned, and I feel that the skirt is too long for walking; sometimes it is certainly too tight to enable a woman to get into an omnibus or railway carriage gracefully. Probable price, complete, $50.

2. For summer wear, a plain blouse and skirt; not the atrocious blouse ending at the belt, but the beautiful tunic-blouse that falls over the hips. Both blouse and skirt would need to be made of a permanently fixed, plain, and uni-colored material. Total cost, $25.

3. If the skirt were shortened, leggings, gaiters, and stockings would have to be standardized; the shoe buckle, being too costly, would disappear.

4. A fixed type of hat, without feathers or aigrettes, made in straw and trimmed with flowers; produced in scores of thousands, it ought not to cost more than $2.50.

5. A fixed type of evening gown, price $24 or $32, without any lace or trimmings, sequins, paillettes; without overlays of flimsies of any kind; no voile, no chiffon, no tulle, no muslin, but a stuff of good quality, hanging in straight folds. Jewelry to be banned.

6. The afternoon dress should be completely suppressed; it responds to no need.

7. The total annual cost would be about $150.

I shall be asked whether this can be done. I think it can. Recently the Queen of Italy created a vogue for coral ornaments among the Roman ladies so as to restore their livelihood to the fishermen of Torre del Greco. That points the way; we do not need sumptuary laws, though, in times to come, when capitalism is nothing but a historical incident, we may have passed through such laws into a fuller freedom. It is enough to decree that any variation from the new standard is bad form. Human beings will break all laws, but they shrink if you tell them that they are infringing the rules of etiquette. There are many men to-day who would like to wear satin and velvet: they dare not because it is bad form. If, therefore, a permanent clothing scheme were established by strong patrons, if it were agreeable to the eye, which is easy to arrange, I believe that fashions could be fixed because it would be known that a woman who went beyond the uniform must either be disreputable or suffer from bad taste.

6

I shall be told that I am warring against art. That is not true: some fashions are beautiful, some are hideous. Who would to-day wear the crinoline? Who would wear the gigot sleeve? They are ugly--but, stay! Are they? Will they not be worn in an adapted form some time within the next generation? They will, because fashions are not works of art; they are only fashions. Women do not adapt the fashions to themselves, they adapt themselves to the fashions, and it is a current joke that even woman's anatomy is adjusted to suit the clothes of the day.

Doubtless I shall be challenged on this, and told that woman's individuality expresses itself in her clothes. That again is not true; the girl with a face like a Madonna will wear a ballet skirt if it comes in, and if she has to "adapt" the ballet skirt to the Madonna idea I should like to know how it is going to be done. Indeed the one thing woman avoids doing is expressing her individuality; she wants what Oscar Wilde called "the holy calm of feeling perfectly dressed", that is, like everybody else, and a little more expensively.

It may be retorted, however, that uniform is not cheap. That again is untrue. When a uniform is standardized, turned out in quantities and never varied, it can be made very cheaply. Men's clothing, which is not fully standardized, is such that no man need spend more than $250 a year. That is the condition I want for women. Of course it will make unemployed, and our sympathy will be invoked for dressmakers thrown out of work: that is the old argument against railways on behalf of coaches, against the mule-jenny, against every engine of human progress, and it is sheer barbarism. Labor redistributes itself; money wasted on women's clothes will be used in other trades which will reabsorb the labor and make it useful instead of sterile.

An apparently more powerful argument is that uniform would deprive women of their individuality: it cannot be much of an individuality that depends upon a frock, and I am reduced to wonder whether some women lose their personality once their frock is taken off. Still, there is a little force in the argument, for it seems to lead to the conclusion that beautiful women will enjoy undue advantage when dressed as are the ill-favored. But this is not a true conclusion; it is not even true to say that one cannot be distinctive in uniform, as anybody will realize who compares a smart soldier with an untidy one. I have myself worn a soldier's coat and know what care may make of it. Nor do I believe that the beautiful would win; by winning is meant winning men, but we know perfectly well that it is not body which wins men: it wins them only to lose them after a while. It is something else which wins men: individuality, wit, gaiety, cleverness, or cleverness clever enough to appear foolish. And we men who wear uniform, does not our individuality manage to attract? It does; and indeed I go further: I assert that fashions smother individuality because they are tyrannical and much more obtrusive than uniforms. Woman's charms are to-day dwarfed because men are dazzled and misled by the meretricious paraphernalia which clothe woman; the true charms have to struggle for life. I want to give them full play, to enable men to choose better and more sanely, no longer the empty odalisque but the woman whose personality is such that it can dominate her uniform. That will be a true race and a finer than the game of sex-temptation which women think they are playing.

It may be said that uniform will do away with class distinctions, that one will no longer be able to tell a lady from one who is not. That is not true. What one will no longer be able to tell is a rich woman from a poor one; and who is to complain of that? Surely it will not be men, for it is not true, I repeat, that men admire extravagant clothes; nor are they tempted by them; nor do women dress to tempt them: at any rate, the seduction of Adam was not compassed in that way.

Besides, women give away their own case: if their clothes were intended to attract men, then surely married women would cease to follow the fashions unless, which I am reluctant to conclude, they still desire to pursue after marriage their nefarious, heart-breaking career.

The last suggestion is that women would not wear the uniform. Not follow a fashion? This has never happened before.

I adhere therefore to my general view that if woman is to be diverted from the path that leads straight toward a greater degradation of her faculties; if household budgets are to be relieved so as to leave money for pleasure and for culture; if true beauty is to take the place of tinsel, feathers, frills, ruffles, poudre de riz; if middle-class women are to cease to live in bitterness because they cannot keep up with the rich; if the daughters of the poor are no longer to be stimulated and corrupted by example into poverty and prostitution, it will be necessary for the few who lead the many to realize that simplicity, modesty, moderation, and grace are the only things which will enable women to gain for themselves, and for men, peace and satisfaction out of a civilization every day more hectic.

IV

WOMAN AND THE PAINT POT

It is in a shrinking spirit that I venture to suggest that woman has so far entirely failed to affirm her capacity in the pictorial arts, for I address myself to an audience which contains many sculptors and pictorial artists, an audience of serious and enthusiastic people to whom art matters as much and perhaps more than life. But it is of no use maintaining illusions; woman has exhibited, and is exhibiting, very great artistic capacities in the histrionic art, in dancing, in executive music, and in literature. There is, therefore, no case for those who argue that woman has no artistic capacity. She has. I select but a few out of the many when I quote the actresses, Siddons, Rachel, La Duse, Sarah Bernhardt, Ellen Terry; the dancers, La Duncan, Pavlova, Gen 閑; the literary women, the Bronte, Madame de Sta 雠, George Eliot, Sappho, Christina Rossetti; among the more modern, May Sinclair and Lucas Malet.

At first sight, however, it is curious that I should be able to quote no composers and no dramatists; it is impossible to take Guy d'Hardelot and Theresa del Riego seriously. And the women dramatists, taken as a whole, hardly exist. This would go to show that there is some strength in the contention that woman is purely executive and uncreative; but this cannot be true, for the list of writers I have given, which is very far from being exhaustive, and which is being augmented every day by promising girl writers, shows that woman has creative capacity, creative in the sense that she can evolve character and scene, and treat relations in that way which can be described as art. If, therefore, there have been no women painters of note, it cannot be because woman has no creative capacity. It may be suggested that those women who have creative capacity turn to literature, but that is a very rash assumption. For creative men turn to any one of the half-dozen forms of art, and are not monopolized by literature; there is no reason, mental or physical, why the female genius should be capable of traveling only along one line. The problem is a problem of direction, a problem of medium.

My potential opponents will probably deny that there have been, and are, no women painters. They will quote the names of Angelica Kaufmann, of Vig 閑-Lebrun, of Rosa Bonheur, of Berthe Morisot, of Elizabeth Butler; the more modern will mention Ella Bedford, Lucy Kemp-Welch; the most modern will put forward Anne Estelle Rice; and one or two may shyly whisper Maude Goodman. But, honestly, does this amount to anything? I do not suppose that Lady Elizabeth Butler's "Inkermann" or "Floreat Etona" will outlive the works of Detaille or of Meissonier, however doubtful be the value of these men; the fame of Angelica Kaufmann, though enhanced by the patronage of kings, has not been perpetuated by Bartolozzi, in spite of that etcher's inflated reputation. Rosa Bonheur's "Horse Fair" hangs in the National Gallery, and another of her works in the Luxembourg, but merits which balance those of Landseer are not enough; and Berthe Morisot walked, it is true, in the footprints of Manet, but did her feet fill them? The truth of the matter is that there has not been a woman Velasquez, a woman Rembrandt.

Now, as some of my readers may know, I do not make a habit of belittling woman and her work. My writings show that I am one of the most extreme feminists of the day, and I am well aware that woman must not be judged upon her past, that it is perhaps not enough to judge her on her present position, and that imagination, the only spirit with which criticism should be informed if it is to have any creative value, should take note of the potentialities of woman. But still, though we may write off much of the past and flout the record of insult and outrage which is the history of woman under the government of man, we cannot entirely ignore the present: the present may not be the father of the future, but it is certainly one of its ancestors. We have to-day a number of women who paint--the great majority, such as Mrs. Von Glehn, Ella Bedford, Lucy Kemp-Welch, and others who are hung a little higher over the line, are rendering Nature and persons with inspired and photographic zeal; others, such as Anne Estelle Rice, Jessie Dismorr, Georges Banks, are inclined to "fling their paint pot into the faces of the public." Some do not abhor Herkomer, others are banded with Matisse; but though to be Herkomer may not be supreme, and though to be Matisse may perhaps be insane, it must regretfully be conceded that the heights of the Royal Academy and of Parnassus (or whatever the painter's mountain may be) are not haunted by the woman painter. Without being carried away by the author of "Bubbles", I am not inclined to be carried away by Maude Goodman and the splendours of "Taller Than Mother." Lucy Kemp-Welch's New Forest ponies are ponies, but I do not suppose that they will be trotting in the next century; they do not balance even the work of Furse.

Let me not be reproached because I use the low standard of the Royal Academy, for if woman has a case at all she must prove herself on all planes; it is as important that she should equal the second-rate people as that she should shine among the first-rate. I do not look for a time to come when woman will be superior to man, but to a time, quite remote enough for my speculations, when she will be his equal, when she will be able to keep up with all his activities. Curiously enough, the advanced female painters are not so inferior to the advanced men painters as are the stereotyped women to their masculine rivals. There is excellence in the work of Anne Estelle Rice and Georges Banks, though they perhaps do not equal Fergusson; but they are less remote from him in spirit and realization than are the lesser women from the lesser men. That is a fact of immense importance, for it is evident that nothing is so hopeful as this reduction in the inferiority of female painting. It may be that masculine painting is decaying, which would facilitate woman's victory, but I do not think so; modern masculine painting has never been so vigorous, so inspired by an idea since the great religious uprush of the Primitives.

Women are striving to conform not to a lower but to a higher standard, a standard where the sensuality of art is informed by intellect. If, therefore, they conform more closely to the standard which men are establishing, they are more than holding their own; they are gaining ground.

Yet they are still, in numbers and in quality, much inferior to the men. Anne Estelle Rice alone cannot tilt in the ring against Fergusson, Gaugin, Matisse, Picasso. And it is not true that they have been entirely deprived of opportunity. Up to the 'seventies or 'eighties, woman was certainly very much hampered by public opinion. For some centuries it had been held that she should paint flowers, but not bodies; nowadays, dizzily soaring, she has begun to paint cranes and gasometers. The result of the old attitude was that the work of women was mainly futile because it was expected to be futile; though painters were not always gentlemen, female painters seemed to have to be ladies, but times changed. There came the djibbah, Bernard Shaw, and the cigarette; women began to flock into Colarossi's and the Slade, into the minor schools where, I regret to say, the new spirit has yet to blow and to do away with the interesting practice of the life class where the male model wears bathing drawers. Woman has had her opportunity, and any morning on the Boulevard Montparnasse you can see her carrying her paraphernalia towards the Grande Chaumi 鑢 e and the other studios. She is suffering a good deal from the effects of past neglect, but much of that neglect is so far away that we must ask ourselves why woman has not yet responded to the more tender attitude of modern days. For she has not entirely responded; she is still either a little afraid of novelty or inclined to hug it, to affront the notorious perils of love at first sight.

I believe that the causes of women's failure in painting are twofold--manual and mental. Though disinclined to generalize upon the female temperament, because such generalizations generally lead to the discovery of a paradox, I am conscious in woman of a quality of impatience.

While woman will exhibit infinite patience, infinite obstinacy, in the pursuit of an end, she is often inclined to leap too quickly towards that end. To use a metaphor, she may spend her whole life in trying to cut down a tree without taking the preliminary trouble to have her ax sharpened; she does unwillingly the immense labor on the antique, she neglects her anatomy, she sacrifices line to color.

This is natural enough, for she has a keen sense of color. As witness her clothes. When clothes are the work of woman they are generally beautiful in color; when they are beautiful in line they are generally by Poiret. For line tends to be pure and cold, and I hope I will shock nobody when I suggest that purity and coldness are masculine rather than feminine. Color is the expression of passion, line is the expression of intellect, or rather of that curious combination of intellect and passion, of intellect directing passion, and of passion inflaming intellect, which is art as understood by man. It is to this second group of causes, those I have called mental, that the inferiority of the woman painter is traceable. There is a lack of intellect in her work. It is true that the male painter is often just a painter, and that I can think of no case to-day which reproduces the engineering capacities of Leonardo da Vinci, but I refer rather to a general intellectual sweep than to a specialized capacity. Men do not hold themselves so far aloof from politics, business and philosophy as do women; too many of the latter read nothing whatever. For some painters a novel is too much, while their selection among the contents of the newspaper might be improved upon by a domestic servant. There is a lack of depth, a lack of intellectual quality, of that "general" quality which, directed into other channels, produces the engineer, the business man and the politician. I do not believe in "artistic capacity", "scientific capacity", "business capacity"; there is nothing but "capacity" which takes varying forms, just as there is red hair and black hair, but always hair. In male painting intellect sometimes stands behind passion; in female painting the attitude is purely sensuous, and that is not to be wondered at: from the days of the anthropoid ape to this one we have developed nothing in woman but the passionate quality; we have taught her to charm, to smile, and to lie until she thinks she can do nothing but charm, and believes in her own lies. We have refused her education, we have made her into a slave. Thus, while many of the male painters are not intellectuals, they have been able to draw upon the higher average quality of the male mind, while woman to-day, desirous of so doing, will find very little to the credit of the account of her sex.

What is the conclusion to be drawn? It is to my mind obvious enough. If woman is producing inferior work it is because she is still an inferior creature, but I do not think she will remain one. Her progress during the last thirty years has been staggering; she has forced herself into the trades, into professions, into politics; she has produced standard works; in one or two cases she has been creative in science; and I believe, therefore, that her intellect is on the up grade, and that her sex is accumulating those resources which will serve as a background to the artistic development of her passionate faculty. Woman is about to gain political power. She will use it to improve the education of her sex, to broaden its opportunities. She is coming out into the world in co 鰌 eration and in conflict with man; she will become more self-conscious, and gain a solidarity of sex upon which will follow mutual mental stimulation and specialized sex development. For that reason I believe woman's progress will not be less in the pictorial arts than in other fields if she develops in herself the fullness of life and its implications. She will inevitably wage the sex war: she will gain her artistic deserts after the sex peace.

V

THE DOWNFALL OF THE HOME

There is something the matter with the home. It may be merely the subtle decay which, in birth beginning and in death persisting, escorts all things human and perchance divine. It may be decay assisted by the violence of a time unborn and striving through novelty toward its own end, or toward an endlessness of change. But, whatever the causes, which interest little a hasty generation, signs written in brick and mortar and social custom, in rebellion and in aspiration, are not wanting to show that the home, so long the center of Anglo-Saxon and American society, is doomed. And, as is usual in the twentieth century, as has been usual since the middle of the nineteenth, woman is at the bottom of the change. It is women who now make revolutions. A hundred years ago it was men who made revolutions; nowadays they content themselves with resolutions. So it has been left for woman, more animal, more radical, more divinely endowed with the faculty of seeing only her own side, to sap the foundations of what was supposed to be her shelter.

I do not suppose that the household has ever been quite as much of a shelter for women as the Victorian philosophers said, and possibly believed; an elementary study of the feminist question will certainly incline the unprejudiced to see that the home, which has for so long masqueraded in the guise of woman's friend, has on the whole been her enemy; that instead of being her protector it has been her oppressor; that it has not been her fortress, but her jail. Woman has felt in the home much as a workman might feel if he were given the White House as a present, told to live in it and keep it clean without help on two dollars a week. If the home be a precious possession, it may very well be a possession bought at too high a price--at the price of youth, of energy, and of enlightenment. The whole attitude of woman toward the home is one of rebellion--not of all women, of course, for most of them still accept that, though all that is may not be good, all that is must be made to do. Resignation, humility, and self-sacrifice have for a thousand generations been the worst vices of woman, but it is apparent that at last aggressiveness and selfishness are developing her toward nobility. She is growing aware that she is a human being, a discovery which the centuries had not made, and naturally she hates her gilded cage.

Woman is tired of a home that is too large, where the third floor gets dirty while she is cleaning the first; of a home that cannot be left lest it should be burglared; of a home where there is always a slate wrong, or a broken window, or a shortage of coal. She is tired of being immolated on the domestic hearth. One of them, neither advanced nor protesting, gave me a little while ago an account of what she called a characteristic day. I reproduce it untouched:

THE DAY OF A REALLY NICE ENGLISHWOMAN

8 A.M.--Early tea; rise; no bath. [The husband has the only bath, and the boiler cannot make another until ten.]

9 A.M.--Breakfast. [The husband takes the only newspaper away to the office.]

9.30 A.M.--Conversation with the cook: hardness of the butcher's meat; difficulty because there are only three eatable animals; degeneration of the butter; grocery and milk problems.

Telephone.--A social engagement is made.

Conversation with the cook resumed: report on a mysterious disease of the kitchen boiler; report on the oil-man; report on the plumber.

Correspondence begun and interrupted by the parlor-maid, who demands a new stock of glass.

Correspondence resumed; interrupted by the parlor-maid's demand for change with which to pay the cleaner.

Rush up-stairs to show which covers are to go.

Correspondence resumed, and interrupted by the telephone: the green-grocer states that some of the vegetables she wants cannot be procured.

Correspondence resumed; interrupted by the nurse, who wishes to change the baby's milk.

Three telephone calls.

Correspondence resumed, and interrupted by the housemaid, who wants new brooms.

11 A.M.--The children have gone; the servants are at work. Therefore:

11-11.15 A.M.--Breathing space.

11.15-11.45 A.M.--Paying bills--electricity, gas, clothes; checking the weekly books, reading laundry circulars.

12 M.--Goes out. It is probably wet [this being England], so, not being very well off, she flounders through mud. Interview with the plumber as to the boiler; shoes for Gladys; glass for the parlor-maid; brooms for the housemaid; forgets various things she ought to have done; these worry her during lunch.

1.30 P.M.--Lunch.

2.30 P.M.--Fagged out, lies down, but--

2.45 P.M.--The husband telephones to tell her to go to the library and get him a book.

3.15 P.M.--Is fitted by the dressmaker. Feels better.

4.30 P.M.--Charming at tea.

5.45 P.M.--Compulsory games with the children.

6.15 P.M.--Ultimatum from the servants: the puppy must be killed for reasons which cannot be specified in an American magazine.

6.30-6.35 P.M.--Literature, art, music, and science. Then dress for dinner.

7.30 P.M.--Charming at dinner. Grand fantasia to entertain the male after a strenuous day in the city. Conversation: golf, business, cutting remarks about other people, and no contradicting.

8.45-9.15 P.M.--Literature, art, music, and science.

Last post: Circulars, bills, invitations to be answered; request from a brother in India to send jam which can be bought only in a suburb fourteen miles distant.

10.30 P.M.--Attempted bath, but the plumber has not mended the boiler, after all.

11 P.M.--Sleep ... up to the beginning of another nice Englishwoman's day.

She may exaggerate, but I do not think so, for as I write these lines three stories of a house hang over my head, and I hear culinary noises below. Being a man, I am supposed to rule all this, but, fortunately, not to govern it. And I am moved to interest when I reflect that in this street of sixty houses, that which is going on in my house is probably multiplied by sixty. I have a vision of those sixty houses, each with its dining room and drawing-room, its four to eight bedrooms, and its basement. There are sixty drawing-rooms in this street, and at 11 A.M. there is not a single human being in them; and at 3 P.M. there is nobody in the sixty dining rooms, except on Sunday, when a few men are asleep in them. And I have horrid visions of our sixty kitchens, our sixty sculleries, our sixty pantries; of our one hundred and fifty servants, and our sixty cooks (and cooks so hard to get and to bear with when you've got them!). And I think of all our dinner sets, of the twelve thousand pieces of crockery which we need in our little street. To think of twelve thousand articles of crockery is to realize our remoteness from the monkey. And the nurses, as they pass, fill me with wonder, for some of them attend one child, some two, while sometimes three children have two nurses--until I wonder what percentage of nurse is really required to keep in order an obviously unruly generation.

Complex, enormous, it is not even cheap. Privacy, the purest jewel humanity can find, seems to be the dearest. This inflated individual home, it is marvelous how it has survived! Like most human institutions, it has probably survived because it was there. It has taken woman's time; it has taken much of her energy, much of her health and looks. Worst of all, it seems to have taken from her some of the consideration to which as a human being she was entitled. Let there be no mistake about that. In spite of proclamations as to the sacredness of the home and the dignity of labor, the fact remains that the domestic man, the kind that can hang a picture straight, is generally treated by male acquaintances with sorrowful tolerance; should he attempt to wash the baby, he becomes the kind of man about whom the comic songs are written. (I may seem rather violent, but I once tried to wash a baby.) So that apparently the dignified occupations of the household are not deemed dignified by man. This is evident enough, for office-cleaners, laundresses, step-girls, are never replaced by men. These are the feminine occupations, the coarse occupations, requiring no special intelligence.

The truth is that the status of domestic labor is low. An exception is made in favor of the cook, but only by people who know what cooking is, which excludes the majority of the world. It is true that of late years attempts have been made to raise the capacity of the domestic laborer by inducing her to attend classes on cooking, on child nurture, etc., but, in the main, in ninety-nine per cent of bourgeois marriages, it is assumed that any fool can run a house. It matters very little whether a fool can run a house or not; what does matter from the woman's point of view is that she is given no credit for efficient household management, and that is one reason why she has rebelled. It does not matter whether you are a solicitor, an archbishop, or a burglar, the savor goes out of your profession if it is not publicly esteemed at its true worth. We have heard of celebrated impostors, of celebrated politicians, but who has ever heard of a celebrated housekeeper?

The modern complaint of woman is that the care of the house has divorced her from growing interests, from literature and, what is more important, from the newspaper, partly from music, entirely from politics. It is a purely material question; there are only twenty-four hours in every day, and there are some things one cannot hustle. One can no more hustle the English joint than the decrees of the Supreme Court. Moreover, and this is a collateral fact, an emptiness has formed around woman; while on the one side she was being tempted by the professions that opened to her, by the interests ready to her hand, the old demands of less organized homes were falling away from her. Once upon a time she was a slave; now she is a half-timer, and the taste of liberty that has come to her has made her more intolerant of the old laws than she was in the ancient days of her serfdom. Not much more than seventy years ago it was still the custom in lower middle-class homes for the woman to sew and bake and brew. These occupations were relinquished, for the distribution of labor made it possible to have them better done at a lower cost.

In the 'fifties and the 'sixties the great shops began to grow, stores to rise of the type of Whiteley and Wanamaker. Woman ceased to be industrial, and became commercial; her chief occupation was now shopping, and if she were intelligent and painstaking she could make a better bargain with Jones, in Queen's Road, than with Smith, in Portchester Street. But of late years even that has begun to go; the great stores dominate the retail trade, and now, qualities being equal, there is hardly anything to pick between universal provider Number 1, at one end of the town, and Number 2, equally universal, at the other. Also the stores sell everything; they facilitate purchases; the housekeeper need not go to ten shops, for at a single one she can buy cheese, bicycles, and elephants. That is only an indication of the movement; the time will come, probably within our lifetime, when the great stores of the towns will have crushed the small traders and turned them into branch managers; when all the prices will be alike, all the goods alike; when food will be so graded that it will no longer be worth the housekeeper's while to try and discover a particularly good sirloin--instead she will telephone for seven pounds of quality AF, Number 14,692. Then, having less to do, woman will want to do still less, and the modern rebellion against house and home will find in her restlessness a greater impetus.

When did the rebellion begin? Almost, it might be said, it began in the beginning, and no doubt before the matriarchate period women were striving toward liberty, only to lose it after having for a while dominated man. In later years women such as Mary Wollstonecraft, but more obscure, strove to emancipate themselves from the thralldom of the household. The aspiration of woman, whether Greek courtesan, French worldling, or English factory inspector, has always been toward equality with man, perhaps toward mastery. And man has always stood in her path to restrict her, to arrest her development for his pleasure, as does to-day the Japanese to the little tree which he plants in a pot. The clamor of to-day against the emancipated woman is as old as the rebukes of St. Paul; Moliere gave it tongue in Les Femmes Savantes, when he made the bourgeois say to his would-be learned wife:

Man has laid down only three occupations: kirche, kohe, kinder.

Hence the revolt. If man had not so much desired that woman should be housekeeper and courtesan, she would not so violently have rebelled against him, for why should one rebel until somebody says, "Thou shalt"! At the words "Thou shalt", rebellion becomes automatic, and, so long as woman has virility in her, so will it be. Still, leaving origins alone, and considering only the last fifty or sixty years of our history, it might be said that they are divided into three periods:

(a) The shiny nose and virtue period.

(b) The powder-puff and possible virtue period.

(c) The Russian ballet and leopard-skin period.

There are exceptions, qualifications, occasional retrogressions, but, taking it roughly, that is the history of English womanhood from wax fruit to Bakst designs. There were crises, such as the early 'eighties, when bloomers came in and women essayed cigarettes, and felt very advanced and sick; when they joined Ibsen clubs and took up Bernard Shaw, and wore eyeglasses and generally tried to be men without succeeding in being gentlemen. There was another crisis about 1906, when suffrage put forward in England its first violent claims. That, too, was abortive in a sense, as is ironically recorded in a comic song popular at the time:

"Back, back to the office she went: The secretary was a perfect gent."

But still, in a rough and general way, there has been a continual and growing discontent with the heavy weight of the household, the complications of its administration. There has been a drive toward freedom which has affected even that most conservative of all animals, the male. There have been conscious rebellions as expressed, for instance, by Nora who "slammed the door"; by the many girls who decide to "live their own lives", as life was expounded in the yellow-backs of the 'nineties; by the growing demand for entry into the professions; for votes; for admission to the legislatures. There is nothing irrelevant in this; given that by the nature of her position in society and of the duties intrusted to her in the household, she was cut off from all other fields of human activity, it may be said that every attempt that woman has made to share in any activity that lay beyond her front door has been revolutionary and directed at the foundations of the English household system. Whether this has also been the case in America, where a curious type of woman has been evolved--pampered, selfish, intelligent, domineering, and wildly pleasure-loving--I cannot tell. Nor is it my business; like other men, the Americans have the wives they deserve.

But behind the conscious rebellions are the subtle and, in a way, infinitely more powerful unconscious rebellions, the dull discontents of overworked and over-preoccupied women; the weariness, the desire for pleasure and travel, for change, for time to play and to love, and--what is more pathetic-- for time just to sit and rest. The epitaph of the charwoman--

"Weep for me not, weep for me never, I'm going to do nothing, nothing forever--"

embodies pains deep-buried in millions of women's hearts. Most people do not know that, because women never smile so brightly as when they are unhappy. Sometimes I suspect that public pronouncements and suffrage manifestoes have had very much less to do with modern upheavals than these slumberous protests against the multiplicity of errands and the intricacies of the kitchen range.

Even man has been affected by the change, has begun to realize that it is quite impossible to alter custom while leaving custom unaltered, which, as anybody knows who reads parliamentary debates, is mankind's dearest desire. Changes in his habits and in his surroundings, such as the weekend, the servant problem, the restaurant, the hotel; all these have been separate disruptive factors, have begun to bring about the downfall of the English household. I do not know that one can assign a predominant place to any one of these factors; they are each one as the drop of water that, joined with its fellows, wears away stone. Moreover, in socio-psychologic investigation it is often found that what appears to be a cause is an effect, and vice versa. For instance, with regard to restaurant dining, it may be that people frequent restaurants because the home cooking is bad, and, on the other hand, it may be that home cooking has become bad because people have neglected it as they found it easier to go to the restaurant. This attitude of mind must qualify the conclusion at which I arrive, and it is an attitude which must be sedulously cultivated by any one who wants to know the truth instead of wishing merely to have his prejudices confirmed.

But, all allowances made, it is perfectly clear that the first group of disruptive factors, such as the restaurant dinner, the week-end, the long and frequent holidays, the motor car, the spread of golf, is inimical to the home idea and, therefore, to the house idea. (Home means house, and does not mean flat, for which see further on.) The home idea is complex; it embraces privacy, possession; it implies a place where one can retreat, be master, be powerful in a small sphere, take off one's boots, be sulky or pleasant, as one likes. It involves, above all, a place where one does not hear the neighbor's piano, or the neighbor's baby, or, with luck, the neighbor's cat; but where, on the other hand, one's own piano, one's own baby, and one's own cat are raised to a high and personal pitch of importance. It involves everything that is individual--one's own stationery block, one's crest, or, if one is not so fortunate, one's monogram upon the plate. If the S.P.C.A. did not intervene, I think one might often see in the front garden a cat branded with a hot iron: "Thomas Jones. His Cat." It is the rallying-point of domestic virtue, the origin of domestic tyranny. It is the place where public opinion cannot see you and where, therefore, you may behave badly. Most wife beaters live in houses; in flats they would be afraid of the opinion of the hall porter. And yet the home is not without its charm and its nobility, for its bricks and mortar enshrine a spirit that is worshiped and for which much may be sacrificed. Cigars have been given up so that the home might have a new coat of paint; amusements, holidays, food sometimes--all these have been sacrificed so that, well railed off from the outside world by a front garden, if possible by a back garden, too--or, still more delightful, far from the next house--a little social cosmos might be maintained. So far has this gone in the north of England that many people who could well afford servants will not have them because, as they say, they cannot bear strangers in the house. And very desirable houses in the suburbs of London, with old, walled gardens, have been given up because it was unbearable to take tea under the eyes of passengers on the top of the motor busses.

The home spirit, however, is not content merely with coats of paint and doilies; it demands mental as well as material worship. It demands importance; it insists that it is home, sweet home, and that there is no place like it (which is one comfort); that it is the last thought of the drowning sailor; that the trapper, lost in the deepest forests of Canada, sees rising in the smoke of his lonely camp fire a delicious vision of Aunt Maria's magenta curtains. It lays down that it is wrong to leave it, quite apart from the question of burglars; it has invented scores of phrases to justify otherwise unpleasant husbands who had "given a good home" to their wives; phrases to censure revolting daughters "who had good homes, and what more could they want?" It has frowned upon everything that was outside itself, for it could not see anything that was not itself. It has hated theaters, concerts, dances, lectures, every form of amusement; and, as it has to bear them, likes to refer to them archly as debauches, or going on the razzle-dazzle, or the ran-dan, according to period. It has powerfully allied itself with the pulpit and, in impious circles, with fancy work and crochet; it has enlisted a considerable portion of the Royal Academy to depict it in various scenes for which the recipe is: One tired man with a sunny smile returning to his home; one delighted wife; suitable number of ebullient children and, inevitably, a dog. The dog varies. In England they generally put in a terrier, in war time a bulldog; in Germany it may be a dachshund; and in other countries it is another kind of dog, but it is always the same idea.

And so it is not wonderful that the home has looked censoriously upon everything that took people away from its orbit. Likewise it is not wonderful that people have fled to anything available so as to escape the charmed circle. The week-end is in general a very over-rated amusement, for it consists mainly in packing and preparing to catch a train, then thinking of packing and catching a train, then packing and catching a train; but still the week-end amounts to a desertion, and hardly a month passes without a divine laying of savage hands upon the excursion. There was a time when holidays themselves were looked upon as audacious breaches of the conventions. In the early nineteenth century nobody went to Brighton except the Regent and the smart set; even in the Thackerayan period people did not think it necessary to leave London in August, and when they took the Grand Tour they were bent on improving their minds. The Kickleburys could not go up the Rhine without a powerful feeling of self-consciousness; I think they felt that they were outraging the Victorian virtues, so they had to make up for it by taking a guide, who for four or five weeks lectured them day and night upon the ruins of Godesberg. All this was opposed to the spirit of the home, just as anything which is outside the home is opposed to the spirit of the home, as was, for instance, every dance that has ever been known. In the Observer, in 1820, appeared a poem expressing horror and disgust of the waltz, and, curiously enough, very much in the same terms as the diatribes in the American papers of 1914 against the turkey trot and the bunny hug. When the polka came in, in the middle of the nineteenth century, good people clustered to see it danced, just like the more recent tango, and it was considered very fast. All this may appear somewhat irrelevant, but my case is mainly that the old attitude, now decaying, is that anything that happened outside the home, whether sport or amusement, was anything between faintly and violently evil. The old ideal of home was concentrated in Sunday: a long night; heavy breakfast; church; walk in the park; heavy dinner, including roast beef; profound sleep in the dining room; heavy tea; then nothing whatever; church; heavy supper; nothing whatever; then sleep. There is not much of this left, and from the moment when Sunday concerts began and the picture galleries were opened, when chess was played and the newspaper read, the old solidities of the home trembled, for the home was an edifice from which one could not take one stone.

In chorus with the cry for new pleasures, the reaction against the old discomfort, came a more powerful influence still, because it was direct--the servant problem. The Americans know this question, I think, better even than the British, for in their country a violent democracy rejects domestic service and compels, I believe, the use of recent emigrants from old enslaved Europe who have not yet breathed the aggressive and ambitious air that has touched the Stars and Stripes. In Great Britain the crisis is not yet, and it may never come, for this is not the English way. In England we are aware of a crisis only fifty years later, because for that half-century we have successfully pretended that there was no crisis. So we come in just in time for the reaction, and say: "There you are. I told you nothing was changed." Yet, so persistent is the servant problem that even England has had to take some notice of it. As Mr. Wells said, the supply of rough, hardworking girls began to shrink. It shrank because so many opportunities for the employment of women were offered by the factories which arose in England in the 'forties and the 'fifties, by the demand for waitresses, for shorthand writers, typists, shopgirls, elementary schoolmistresses, etc. The Education Act of 1870 gave the young English girls of that day a violent shock, for it informed them of the existence of Paris, assisted them toward the piano. And then came the development of the factory system, the spread of cheapness; with the rise in wages came a rising desire for pretty, cheap things almost as pretty as the dear ones; substitutes for costly stuffs were found; compositions replaced ivory, mercerized cotton rivaled silk, and little by little the young girl of the people discovered that with a little cleverness she could look quite as well as the one whom her mother called "Madam"; so she ceased to call her "Madam." Labor daily grows more truculent, so there is no knowing what she will call the ex-Madam next; but one thing is certain, and that is that she will not serve her. She will not, because she looks upon service as ignominious; she has her own pride; she will not tell you that she is in a shop, but that she is "in business"; if she is "in service", often she will say nothing about it at all, for the other girls, who work their eleven hours a day for a few shillings a week, despise her. They at least have fixed hours and they do not "live in"; when they have done their work they are free. They may have had less to eat that day than the comfortable parlor-maid, and maybe they have less in their pockets, but they are free, and they do not hesitate to show their contempt to the helot. I think that new pride has done as much as anything to crush the old, large, unwieldy home, for its four stories and its vast basement needed many steady, hardworking slaves, who only spoke when they were spoken to and always obeyed. It is not that mistresses were bad; some were and some were not, but from the modern girl's point of view they were all bad because they had power at any time of day or night to demand service, to impose tasks that were not contracted for, to forbid the house to the servant's friends, to make her loves difficult, to forbid her even to speak to a man. Whether the mistress so behaved did not matter; she had the power, and in a society growingly individual, growingly democratic, that was bound to become a heavy yoke.

And so, very slowly, the modern evolution began. The first to go were the immense houses of Kensington, Paddington, Bayswater, Bloomsbury,--those old houses within hail of Hyde Park,--which once held large families, all of them anxious to live not too far from the Court. They fell because it was almost impossible to afford enough servants to keep in order their three or four reception rooms, and their eight, ten, twelve bedrooms; they fell because the birth rate shrank, and the large families of the early nineteenth century became exceptional; they fell also because the old rigidity, or rather the stateliness, of the home was vanishing; because the lady of the house ventured to have tea in her drawing-room when there were no callers, and little by little came to leave newspapers about in it and to smoke in it. With the difficulties of the old houses came a demand for something smaller, requiring less labor. This accounts for the villas, of which some four hundred thousand have been built in the suburbs of London, in the villages London has absorbed. They are atrocious imitations of the most debased Elizabethan style; they show concrete where they should use stone, but, as their predecessors showed stucco, they are not much worse. They exhibit painted black stripes where there should be beams; they have sloping roofs, gables, dormer windows, everything cunningly arranged to make as many corners as possible where no chair can stand. They have horrid little gardens where the builder has buried many broken bricks, sardine tins, and old hats; they represent the taste of the twentieth century; they are quite abominable. But still the fact remains that they are infinitely smaller, more manageable, more intelligently planned than the spacious old houses of the past, where every black cupboard bred the cockroach and the mouse. They are easy to warm and easy to clean; their windows are not limited by the old window tax; they have bathrooms even when their rent is only one hundred and fifty dollars a year; and especially they have no basement. The disappearance of the basement is one of the most significant aspects of the downfall of the old household, for it was essentially the servants' floor, where they could be kept apart from their masters, maintaining their own sports and the mysterious customs of a strange people; when the door of the kitchen stairs was shut, one would keep out everything connected with the servants, except perhaps the smell of the roast leg of mutton. That did not matter, for that was homelike. The basement was a vestige of feudal English society; it was brother to the servants' quarters and the servants' hall. Now it is gone. In many places the tradesmen's entrance has vanished, and the cabbage comes to the front door. The sacred suppressions are no more, and in a developing democracy the master and mistress of the house stately dine, while on the other side of a wall about an inch thick Jane can be heard conversing with the policeman.

The growth of the small house has never stopped during the last forty or fifty years. A builder in the southwest of London, of whom I made inquiries, told me that he had erected four hundred and twenty houses, and that not one of them had a basement; this form of architecture had not even occurred to him. I have also visited very many homes in the suburbs of London, and I have looked in vain for the old precincts of the serving maid. The small house has powerfully affected the old individual attitude of home, for the hostile dignity of the past cannot survive when one man mows the lawn and the other clips the roses, each in his own garden, separated only by three sticks and some barbed wire. In detached houses it is worse, for they are now so close together that in certain architectural conditions preliminaries are required before one can take a private bath. The whole direction of domestic architecture is against the individual and for the group. The modern home takes away even the old stores; there are no more pickle cupboards and jam cupboards, and hardly linen cupboards. Why should there be when jam and pickles come from the grocer, and few men have more than twelve shirts? There is not even a store for coal. Some years ago I lived in a house that was built in 1820, and its coal cellar held eight tons; I now inhabit one, built in 1860, in which I can accommodate four tons; the house now being built in the suburbs cannot receive more than one ton. The evolution of the coal cellar is a little the evolution of English society from the time when every man had to live a good deal for himself, until slightly better distribution made it possible for him to combine with his fellows. He need not now store coal, for there is a service of coal to his doorstep. Besides, the offspring of coal are expelling their ancestor; gas and electricity, both centrally supplied from a single source, are sapping the old hearthstone that was fed by one small family, and for that family alone glowed. A continual socialization has come about, and it is not going to stop. What is done in common is on the whole better done, more cheaply done. But what is done in common is hostile to the old home spirit, because the principle of the home spirit is that anything done in common is--well, common!

As for the old houses of fifteen to sixteen rooms, they have had to accommodate themselves to the new conditions. First they tried to maintain themselves by reducing their rents. I know of a case, in Courtfield Gardens, where a house leased twenty-six years ago at one thousand dollars a year, was leased again about ten years ago at seven hundred and fifty dollars a year, and is now being offered at five hundred dollars a year. The owner does not want his premises turned into a boarding house, but he cannot find a private tenant, because hardly anybody nowadays can manage five floors and a basement. In my own district, where the houses tower up to heaven, I see the process at work,--rents falling, pitiful attempts of the landlords to prevent their houses from turning into maisonnettes and boarding houses, to prevent the general decay. But they are beaten. The vast Victorian houses within three miles of Charing Cross are, one by one, being cut up into flats; in the unfashionable districts they are being used for tenements; and there are splendid old houses in the neighborhood of Bloomsbury, where in the day of Dickens lived the fashionables, which now house half a dozen workingclass families and their lodgers. There is one of these old glories near Lamb's Conduit Street, where a Polish furrier and his six unwashed assistants work under a ceiling sown with sprawling nymphs, while melancholic and chipped golden lions' heads look down from either side of a once splendid Georgian mantelpiece. It is very reactionary of me, I am afraid, but I cannot help feeling it a pity that this old house, where would suitably walk the ghost of Brinsley Sheridan, must be one of the eggs broken to make the omelette of the future.

But these old houses must go. Why should one preserve an old house? One does not preserve one's old boots. The old houses have been seized by the current of revolt against the home; they have mostly become boarding and apartment houses. This is not only because their owners do not know what to do with them; one does not run a boarding house unless it pays, and so evidently there has been a growing demand for the boarding house. Boarding houses fail, but for every one that fails two rise up, and there is hardly a street in London that has not its boarding house, or at least its apartment house. There are several in Park Lane itself; there is even one whose lodgers may look into the gardens of Buckingham Palace. I do not know how many boarding houses there are in London, for no statistics distinguish properly between the boarding house, the apartment house, the private hotel, the hotel, and the tavern. But, evidently, the increase is continuous, and part of the explanation is to be found elsewhere than in the traveler. Of course, the traveler has enormously increased, but he alone cannot account for the scores of thousands of people who pass their years in apartment and boarding houses. They live there for various reasons--because they cling to the old family idea and think to find "a home from home"; because they cannot afford to run separate establishments; and very many because they are tired of running them, tired of the plumber, tired of the housemaid. There are thousands of families in London, quite well-to-do, who prefer to live in boarding houses; they hate the boarding house, but they hate it less than home. They feel less tied; they have less furniture; they like to feel that their furniture is in store where they can forget all about it. They have lost part of their old love for Aunt Maria's magenta curtains--the home idea has become less significant to them. And this applies also to hotels. The increase of hotels in London, in every provincial city, all over the world, is not entirely explained by the traveler, though, by the way, the increase in traveling is a sign of the decay of the home. The old idea, "You've got a good home and you've got to stay there," suffers whenever a member of the home leaves it for any reason other than the virtuous pursuit of his business. All over the center of London, in Piccadilly, along Hyde Park, in Bloomsbury, hotels have risen--the Piccadilly, the new Ritz, the Park View, the Coburg, the Cadogan, the Waldorf, the Jermyn Court, the Marble Arch, so many that in some places they are beginning to form a row. And still they rise. An enormous hotel is being built opposite Green Park; another is projected at Hyde Park Corner; the Strand Palace is open, and at the Regent Palace there are, I understand, fourteen hundred bedrooms. The position is that a proportion of London's population is beginning to live in these hotels without servants of their own, without furniture of their own, without houses of their own. A more detached, a freer spirit is invading them, and a desire to get all they can out of life while they can, instead of solemnly worshiping the Englishman's castle.

It does not come easily, and it does not come quickly. During the last twenty-five years most of the blocks of flats to be found in London have risen, with their villainously convenient lifts for passengers and their new-fangled lifts for dust bins and coal, with their electricity and their white paint, and other signs of emancipation. They were not popular when they came, and they are disliked by the older generation; it is still a little vicious to live in a West End flat. And when the younger generation points out that flats are so convenient because you can leave them, the older generation shakes its head and wonders why one should want to. In a future, which I glimpse clearly enough, I see many more causes of disquiet for the older generation, and I wonder with a certain fear whether I, too, shall not be dismayed when I become the older generation. For the destruction of the old home is extending now much farther than bricks and mortar. It is touching the center of human life, the kitchen. There are now in London quite a number of flats, such as, I think, Queen Anne's Mansions, St. James's Court, Artillery Mansions, where the tenants live in agreeable suites and either take their meals in the public restaurant or have them brought up to their flat. The difficulty of service is being reduced. The sixty households are beginning to do without the sixty cooks, and never use more than a few dozen at a time of their two hundred pieces of crockery. There are no more tradesmen, nor is there any ordering; there is a menu and a telephone. There are no more heated interviews with the cook, and no more notices given ten minutes before the party, but a chat with a manager who has the manners and the tact of an ambassador. There is no more home work in these places.

I think these blocks of flats point the way to the future much more clearly than the hotels and the boarding houses, for those are only makeshifts. Generally speaking, boarding houses are bad and uncomfortable, for the landlady is sometimes drunk and generally ill-tempered, the servants are usually dirty and always overworked; the furniture clamors for destruction by the city council. The new system--blocks of flats with a central restaurant--will probably, in a more or less modified form, be the home of new British generations. I conceive the future homes of the people as separate communities, say blocks of a hundred flats or perhaps more, standing in a common garden which will be kept up by the estate. Each flat will probably have one room for each inhabitant, so as to secure the privacy which is very necessary even to those who no longer believe in the home idea; it will also have a common room where privacy can be dispensed with. Its furniture will be partly personal, but not very, for a movement which is developing in America will extend, and we too in England may be provided, as are to-day the more fortunate Americans, with an abundance of cupboards and dressers ready fixed to the walls. There will be no coal, but only electricity and gas, run from the central plant. There will be no kitchens, but one central kitchen, and a central dining room, run--and this is very important--by a committee of tenants.

That committee will appoint and control cooks and all servants; it will buy all provisions, and it will buy them cheaply, for it will purchase by the hundredweight. It will control the central laundry, and a paid laundry maid will check the lists--there will no longer be, as once upon a time on Saturday evenings, a hundred persons checking a hundred lists. It is even quite possible that the central organization may darn socks. The servants will no longer be slaves, personally attached to a few persons, their chattel; they will be day workers, laboring eight hours, without any master save their duty. The whole system of the household will be grouped for the purpose of buying and distributing everything that is needed at any hour. There will be no more personal shopping; the wholesale cleaner will call on certain days without being told to; the communistic window cleaners will dispose of every window on a given day; there may even be in the garden a communistic system of dog kennels. I have no proposal for controlling cats, for I understand that no man can do that ... but then there will be no mice in those days.

I think I will close upon that phrase: There will be no mice in those days. For somehow the industrious mouse, scuffling behind the loose wainscoting over the rotten boards, is to me curiously significant of the old, hostile order, when every man jealously held what was his own and determined that it should so remain--dirty, insanitary, tiresome, labor-making, dull, inexpressibly ugly, inexpressibly inimical to anything fresh and free, providing that it was wholly and sacredly his own.

VI

THE BREAK-UP OF THE FAMILY

1

As with the home, so with the family. It would be strange indeed if a stained shell were to hold a sound nut. All the events of the last century--the development of the factory system, the Married Women's Property Act, the birth of Mr. Bernard Shaw, the entry of woman into professions, the discovery of co-education and of education itself, eugenics, Christian Science, new music halls and halfpenny papers, the Russian ballet, cheap travel, woman suffrage, apartment houses--all this change and stress has lowered the status of one whom Pliny admired--the father of a family. The family itself tends to disappear, and it is many years since letters appeared in The Times over the signature, "Mother of Six." The family is smaller, and, strangely enough, it is sweeter tempered: would it be fair to conclude, as might an Irishman, that it would agree perfectly if it disappeared?

I do not think that the family will completely disappear any more than scarlet fever or the tax collector. But certainly it will change in character, and its evolution already points toward its new form. The old-fashioned family sickened because it was a compulsory grouping. The wife cleaved unto her husband because he paid the bills; the children cleaved unto their parents because they must cleave unto something. There was no chance of getting out, for there was nothing to get out to. For the girl, especially, some fifty years ago, to escape from the family into the world was much the same thing as burgling a penitentiary; so she stayed, compulsorily grouped. Personally, I think all kinds of compulsory groupings bad. If one is compelled to do a thing, one hates it; possibly the dead warriors in the Elysian Fields have by this time taken a violent dislike to compulsory chariot races, and absolutely detest their endless rest on moss-grown banks and their diet of honey. I do not want to stress the idea too far, but I doubt whether the denizens of the Elysian Fields, after so many centuries, can tolerate one another any more, for they are compelled to live all together in this Paradise, and nothing conceivable will ever get them out.

Some groupings are worse than others, and I incline to think that difference of age has most to do with the chafe of family life. For man is a sociable animal; he loves his fellows, and so one wonders why he should so generally detest his relations. There are minor reasons. Relationship amounts to a license to be rude, to the right to exact respect from the young and service from the old; there is the fact that, however high you may rise in the world, your aunt will never see it. There is also the fact that if your aunt does see it, she brags of it behind your back and insults you about it to your face. There is all that, but still I believe that one could to a certain extent agree with one's relations if one met only those who are of one's own age, for compulsory groupings of people of the same age are not always unpleasant; boys are happiest at school, and there is fine fellowship and much merriment in armies. On the other hand, there often reigns a peculiar dislike in offices. I do not want to conclude too rashly, but I cannot help being struck by the fact that in a school or in an army the differences of age are very small, while in an office or a family they are considerable. Add on to the difference of age compulsory intercourse, and you have the seeds of hatred.

This applies particularly where the units of a family are adult. The child loves the grown-ups because he admires them; a little later he finds them out; still a little later, he lets them see that he has found them out, and then family life begins. In many cases it is a quite terrible life, and the more united the family is the more it resembles the union between the shirt of Nessus and Hercules's back. But it must be endured because we have no alternative. I think of cases: of such a one as that of a father and mother, respectively sixty-five and sixty, who have two sons, one of whom ran away to Australia with a barmaid, while the other lived on his sisters' patrimony and regrettably stayed at home; they have four daughters, two of whom have revolted to the extent of earning their living, but spend the whole of their holidays with the old people; the other two are unmarried because the father, imbued with the view that his daughters were too good for any man, refused to have any man in the house. There is another couple in my mind, who have five children, four of whom live at home. I think I will describe this family by quoting one of the father's pronouncements: "There's only one opinion in this house, and that's mine!" I think of other cases, of three sisters who have each an income of two hundred dollars a year on which they would, of course, find it very difficult to live separately. The total income of six hundred dollars a year enables them to live--but together. The eldest loves cats; the next hates cats, but loves dogs; this zo 鰈 ogical quarrel is the chief occupation of the household; the third sister's duty is to keep the cats and dogs apart. Here we have the compulsory grouping; I believe that this lies at the root of disunion in that united family.

The age problem is twofold. It must not be thought that I hold a brief against old age, though, being myself young, I tend to dislike old age as I shall probably dislike youth by and by. On the whole, the attitude of old age is tyrannical. I have heard dicta as interesting as the one which I quote a few lines above. I have heard say a mother to a young man, "You ought to feel affection for me"; another, "It should be enough for you that this is my wish." That is natural enough. It is the tradition of the elders, the Biblical, Greek, Roman, savage hierarchies which, in their time, were sound because, lacking education of any kind, communities could resort only to the experience of the aged. But a thing that is natural is not always convenient, and, after all, the chief mission of the civilizer is to bottle up Nature until she is wanted. This tyranny breeds in youth a quite horrible hatred, while it hardens the old, makes them incapable of seeing the point of view of youth because it is too long since they held it. They insist upon the society of the young; they take them out to call on old people; they drive them round and round the park in broughams, and then round again; they deprive them of entertainments because they themselves cannot bear noise and late hours, or because they have come to fear expense, or because they feel weak and are ill. It is tragic to think that so few of us can hope to die gracefully.

The trouble does not lie entirely with the old; indeed, I think it lies more with the young, who, crossed and irritated, are given to badgering the old people because they are slow, because they do not understand the problems of Lord Kitchener and are still thinking of the problems of Mr. Gladstone. They are harsh because the old are forgetful, because their faded memories are sweet, because they will always prefer the late Sir Henry Irving to Mr. Charles Hawtrey. The young are cruel when the old people refuse to send a letter without sealing it, or when they insist upon buying their hats from the milliner who made them in 1890 and makes them still in the same fashion. They are even harsh to them when they are deaf or short-sighted and fumbling; they come to think that a wise child should learn from his sire's errors.

It is a pity, but thus it is; so what is the use of thinking that the modern family must endure? It is no use to say that the old are right or that the young are right; they disagree. It is nobody's fault, and it is everybody's misfortune. They disagree largely because there is too much propinquity. It is propinquity that brings one to think there is something rather repulsive in blood relations. It is propinquity that brings one to love and then later to dislike. Mr. George Moore has put the case ideally in his Memoirs of My Dead Life, where Doris, the girl who has escaped from her family with the hero says: "This is the first time I have ever lived alone, that I have ever been free from questions. It was a pleasure to remember suddenly, as I was dressing, that no one would ask me where I was going; that I was just like a bird myself, free to spring off the branch and to fly. At home there are always people round one; somebody is in the dining room, somebody is in the drawing-room; and if one goes down the passage with one's hat on, there is always somebody to ask where one is going, and if you say you don't know, they say: 'Are you going to the right or to the left? Because, if you are going to the left, I should like you to stop at the apothecary's and to ask....'"

Yes, that is what happens. That is the tragedy of the family; it lives on top of itself. The daughters go too much with their mothers to shop; there are too many joint holidays, too many compulsory rejoicings at Christmas or on birthdays. There are not enough private places in the house. I have heard one young suffragist, sentenced to fourteen days for breaking windows, say that, quite apart from having struck a blow for the Cause, it was the first peaceful fortnight she had ever known. This should not be confounded with the misunderstood offer of a wellknown leader of the suffrage cause who offered a pound to the funds of the movement for every day that his wife was kept in jail.

In a family, friendships are difficult, for Maude does not always like Arabella's dearest friend; or, which is worse, Maude will stand Arabella's dearest friend, whom she detests, so that next day she may have the privilege of forcing upon Arabella her own, whom Arabella cannot bear. That sort of thing is called tolerance and self-sacrifice; in reality it is mutual tyranny, and amounts to the passing on of pinches, as it were, from boy to boy on the benches of schools. In a developing generation this cannot endure; youthful egotism will not forever tolerate youthful arrogance. As for the old, they cannot indefinitely remain with the young, for, after all, there are only two things to talk of with any intensity--the future and the past; they are the topics of different generations.

Still, for various reasons, this condition is endured. It is cheaper to live together; it is more convenient socially; it is customary, which, especially in England, is most important. But it demands an impossible and unwilling tolerance, sometimes fraudulent exhibitions of love, sometimes sham charity. It is not pleasant to hear Arabella, returning from a walk with her father, say to Maude: "Thank Heaven, that's over! Your turn to-morrow." Perhaps it would not be so if the father did not by threat or by prayer practically compel his daughters to "take duty." There are alleviations--games, small social pleasures, dances--but there is no freedom. A little for the sons, perhaps, but even they are limited in their comings and goings if they live in their father's house. As for the girls, they are driven to find the illusion of freedom in wage labor, unless they marry and develop, as they grow older, the same problem.

2

Fortunately, and this may save something of the family spirit, times are changing. It must not be imagined from the foregoing that I am a resolute enemy of any grouping between men and women, that I view with hatred the family in a box at the theater or round the Sunday joint. I am not attracted by the idea of family; a large family collected together makes me think a little of a rabbit hutch. But I recognize that couples will to the end want to live together, that they will be fond of their children, and that their children will be fond of them; also that it is not socially convenient for husband and wife to live in separate blocks of flats and to hand over their children to the county council. There are a great many children to-day who would be happier in the workhouse than in their homes, but there exists in the human mind a prejudice against the workhouse, and social psychology must take it into account. All I ask is that members of a family should not scourge one another with whips and occasionally with scorpions, and I conceive that nothing could be more delightful than a group of people, not too far removed from one another by age, banded together for mutual recreation and support. So anything that tends to liberalize the family, to exorcise the ghost of the old patriarch, is agreeable.

Patriarch! What a word--the father as master! He will not be master very long, and I do not think that he will want to remain master, for his attitude is changing, not as swiftly as that of his children, but still changing. He is not so sure of himself now when he doubts the advisability of pulling down the shed at the back of the garden, and his youngest daughter quotes from Nietzsche that to build a sanctuary you must first destroy a sanctuary. And, though he is rather uncomfortable, he does not say much when in the evening his wife appears dressed in a Russian ballet frock or even a little less. He is growing used to education, and he fears it less than he did. In fact, he is beginning to appreciate it.

His wife is more suspicious, for she belongs to a generation of women that was ignorant and reveled in its ignorance and called it charm, a generation when all women were fools except the spitfires and the wits. She tends to think that she was "finished" as a lady; her daughters consider that she was done for. The grandmother is a little jealous, but the mother of to-day, the formed woman of about thirty-five, has made a great leap and resembles her children much more than she does her mother. Her offspring do not say: "What is home without a mother? Peace, perfect peace." She is a little too conscientious, perhaps; she has turned her back rather rudely upon her mother's pursuits, such as tea and scandal, and has taken too virulently to lectures or evolution and proteid. She is too vivid, like a newly painted railing, but, like the railing, she will tone down. She pretends to be very socialistic or very fast; on the whole she affects rather the fast style. We must not complain. Is not brown paint in the dining room worse than pink paint on the face?

Whatever may be said about revolting daughters, I suspect that the change in the parent has been greater than that in the child, because the child in 1830 did not differ so much from the child of to-day as might appear. Youth then was restless and insurgent, just as it is to-day; only it was more effectively kept down. If to-day it is less kept down, this is partly for reasons I will indicate, but largely because the adult has changed. The patriarch is nearly dead; he is no longer the polygamous brute who ruled his wives with rods, murdered his infant sons, and sold his infant daughters; his successor, the knight of the Middle Ages, who locked up his wife in a tower for seven years while he crusaded in the Holy Land--he, too, has gone. And the merchant in broadcloth of Victorian days, who slept vigorously in the dining room on Sunday afternoon, has been replaced by a man who says he is sorry if told he snores. He is more liberal; he believes in reason now rather than in force, and generally would not contradict Milton's lines--

"Who overcomes by force Hath overcome but half his foe."

He has come to desire love rather than power, and, little by little--thanks mainly to the "yellow" press--has acquired a chastened liking for new ideas. The spread of pleasure all round him, the vaudeville, the theaters, moving-picture shows, excursions to the seaside--all these have taught him that gaiety may not clash with respectability. Especially, he is more ready to argue, for a peaceful century has taught him that a word is better than a blow. There may be a change in his psychology after this war, for he is being educated by the million in the point of view that a loaded rifle is worth half a dozen scraps of paper; it is quite possible that he will carry this view into his social life. There may, therefore, be a reaction for thirty years or so, but thirty years is a trifle in questions such as these.

Naturally, women have in this direction developed further than men, for they had more leeway to make up. Man has so long been the educated animal that he did not need so much liberalizing. I do not refer to the Middle Ages, when learning was entirely pre 雎 pted by the male (with the exception of poetry and music), for in those days there was no education save among the priests. I mean rather that the great development of elementary learning, which took place in the middle of the nineteenth century, affected men for about a generation before it affected women. In England, at least, university education for women is very recent, for Girton was opened only in 1873, Newnham, at Cambridge, in 1875; Miss Beale made Cheltenham College a power only a little later, and indeed it may be said that formal education developed only about 1890. Both in England and in the United States women have not had much more than a generation to make up the leeway of sixty centuries. It has benefited them as mothers because they did not start with the prejudices left in the male mind by the slow evolution from one form of learning to another; women did not have to live down Plato, Descartes, or Adam Smith; they began on Haeckel and H. G. Wells. The mothers of to-day have been flung neck and crop into Paradise; they came in for the new times, which are always better than the old times and inferior only to to-morrow. They were made to understand a possible democracy in the nursery because all round them, even in Russia, even in Turkey, democracy was growing, some say as a rose, some say as a weed, but anyhow irrepressibly. Who could be a queen by the cradle when more august thrones were tottering? So woman quite suddenly became more than a pretty foil to the educated man, she became something like his superior and his elder; little by little she has begun to teach him who once was her master and still in fond delusion believes he is.

It cannot be said that the mother has until very recently liked education. She has suffered from the prejudice that afflicted her own mother, who thought that because she had worked samplers all girls must work samplers; the "old" woman's daughter, because she went to Cheltenham, tends to think that her little girl ought to go to Cheltenham. It is human rather than feminine, for generations follow one another at Eton and at Harvard. But more than feminine, I think it is masculine because, until very recently, woman has disliked education, while man has treated it with respect; he has not loved it for its own sake, but because he thought that nam et ipsa scientia potestas est. Not a very high motive, but still the future will preoccupy itself very little with the reasons for which we did things; it will be glad enough if we do them. Perhaps we may yet turn the edges of swords on the blasts of rhetoric.

An immediate consequence of the growth of education has been a change in the status of the child. It is no longer property, for how can one prevent a child from pulling down the window sash at night when it knows something of ventilation? Or give it an iron tonic when it realizes that full-blooded people cannot take iron? The child has changed; it is no longer the creature that, pointing to an animal in the field, said, "What's that?" and the reply being, "A cow", asked "Why?" The child is perilously close to asking whether the animal is carnivorous or herbivorous. That makes coercion very difficult. But I do not think that the modern parent desires to coerce as much as did his forbear. Rather he desires to develop the child's personality, and in its early years this leads to horrid results, to children being "taught to see the beautiful" or "being made to realize the duties of a citizen." We are in for a generation made up half of bulbous-headed, bespectacled precocities, and half of barbarians who are "realizing their personality" by the continual use of "shall" and "shan't." This will pass as all things pass, the old child and the rude child, just like the weak parent after the brute parent, and it is enough that the new generation points to another generation, for there seldom was a time that was not better than its father and the herald of a finer son.

Generally the parent will help, for his new attitude can be expressed in a phrase. He does not say, "I am master", but, "I am responsible." He has begun to realize that the child is not a regrettable accident or a little present from Providence; he is beginning to look upon the care of the child as a duty. He has extended the ideal of citizenship, born in the middle of the nineteenth century, which was "to leave the world a little better than he found it"; he has passed on to wanting his son to be a little richer than he was, and a little more learned; he is coming to want his son to be a finer and bolder man; he will come in time to want his daughter to be a finer and bolder woman, which just now he bears pretty well. His wife is helping him a great deal because she is escaping from her home ties to the open trades and professions, to the entertainments of psychic, political, and artistic lectures which make of her head a waste paper basket of intellect, but still create in that head a disturbance far better than the ancient and cow-like placidity. The modern mother is often too much inclined to weigh the baby four times a day, to feed it on ozoneid, or something equally funny, to expose as much of its person as possible, to make it gaze at Botticelli prints when in its bath. She will no doubt want it to mate eugenically, in which she will probably be disappointed, for love laughs at Galtons; but still, in her struggle against disease and wooden thinking, she will have helped the child by giving it something to discard better than the old respects and fears. The modern mother has begun to consider herself as a human being as well as a mother; she no longer thinks that

"A mother is a mother still, The holiest thing alive."

She is coming to look upon herself as a sort of 鉦 thetic school inspector. She lives round her children rather than in them; she is less animal. Above all, she is more critical. Having more opportunity of mixing with people, she ceases to see her child as marvelous because it is her child. She is losing something of her conceit and has learned to say, "the baby" instead of "my baby." It is a revolutionary atmosphere, and the developing child has something to push against when it wants to earn its parents' approval, for modern parents are fair judges of excellence; they are educated. The old-time father was nonplussed by his son, and could not help him in his delectus, but the modern father is not so puzzled when his son wishes to converse of railway finance. The parent, more capable of comradeship, has come to want to be a comrade. He is no longer addressed as "sir"; he is often addressed as "old chap." That is fine, but it is in dead opposition to the close, hard family idea.

Likewise, man and wife have come to look upon each other rather differently; not differently enough, but then humanity never does anything enough; when it comes near to anything drastic it grows afraid. Man still thinks that "whoso findeth a wife findeth a good thing", but he is no longer finding the one he sought not so long ago. She is no longer his property, and it would not occur to the roughest among us to offer a wife for sale for five shillings in Smithfield market, as was done now and then as late as the early nineteenth century. Woman is no longer property; she has been freed; in England she has even been allowed, by the Married Women's Property Act, to hold that which was her own. The Married Women's Property Act has modified the attitude of the mother to her child and to her husband. She is less linked when she has property, for she can go. If every woman had means, or a trade of her own, we should have achieved something like free alliance; woman would be in the position of the woman in "Pygmalion", whom her man could not beat because, she not being married to him, if he beat her she might leave him--in its way a very strong argument against marriage.

But most women have no property, and yet, somehow, by the slow loosening of family links, they have gained some independence. I am not talking of America, where men have deposited their liberty and their fortunes into the prettiest, the greediest, the most ruthless hands in the world; but rather of England, where for a long time a man set up in life with a dog as a friend, a wife to exercise it, and a cat to catch the mice. Until recently the householder kept a tight hand upon domestic expenditure; he paid all the bills, inspected the weekly accounts with a fierce air and an internal hope that he understood them; rent, taxes, heat, light, furniture, repairs, servants' wages, school fees--he saw to it that every penny was accounted for and then, when pleased, gave his wife a tip to go and buy herself a ribbon with. (There are still a great many men who cannot think of anything a woman may want except a ribbon; in 1860 it was a shawl.) When a woman had property, even for some time after the Act, she was not considered fit to administer it. She was not fit, but she should have been allowed to administer it so as to learn from experience how not to be swindled. Anyhow, the money was taken from her, and I know of three cases in a single large family where the wife meekly indorses her dividend warrant so that the husband may pay it into his banking account. That spirit survives, but every day it decays; man, finding his wife competent, tends to make her an allowance, to let her have her own banking account, and never to ask for the pass book. He has thrown upon her the responsibility for all the household and its finance; by realizing that she was capable he has made her capable. Though she be educated, he loves her not less; perhaps he loves her more. It is no longer true to say with Lord Lyttleton that "the lover in the husband may be lost." Formerly the lover was generally lost, for after she had had six children before she was thirty the mother used to put on a cap and retire. Now she does not retire; indeed, she hides his bedroom slippers and puts out his pumps, for life is more vivid and exterior now; this is the cinema age.

Finding her responsible, amusing, capable of looking after herself, man is developing a still stranger liberalism; he has recognized that he may not be enough to fill a woman's life, that she may care for pleasures other than his society, and indeed for that of other men. He has not abandoned his physical jealousy and will not so long as he is a man, but he is slowly beginning to view without dismay his wife's companionship with other men. She may be seen with them; she may lunch with them; she may not, as a rule, dine with them, but that is an evolution to come. This springs from the deep realization that there are between men and women relations other than the passionate. It is still true that between every man and every woman there is a flicker of love, just a shadow, perhaps; but not so long ago between men and women there was only "yes" or "no," and to-day there are also common tastes and common interests. This is fine, this is necessary, but it is not good for the old British household where husband and wife must cleave unto each other alone; where, as in the story books, they lived happy ever after. As with the home, so with the family; neither can survive when it suffers comparison, for it derives all its strength from its exclusivism. As soon as a woman begins to realize that there is charm in the society of men other than her uncles, her brothers, and her cousins, the solid, four-square attitude of the family is menaced. Welcome the stranger, and legal hymen is abashed.

All this springs from woman's new estate--that of human being. She must be considered almost as much as a man. Where there is wealth her tastes must be consulted, and more than one man has been sentenced by a tyrannous wife to wear blue coats and blue ties all his life. She is coming to consider that the husband who dresses in his wife's bedroom should be flogged, while the one who shaves there should be electrocuted. And she defends her view with entirely one-sided logic and an extended vocabulary. Here again is a good, a necessary thing; but where is the old family where a husband could in safety, when slightly overcome, retire to bed with his boots on? He is no longer king of the castle, but a menaced viceroy in an insurgent land.

All through society this loosening of the marriage bond is operative. By being freer within matrimony men and women view more tolerantly breaches of the matrimonial code. There was a time when a male co-respondent was not received: that is over. In those days a divorc 閑 was not received either, even when the divorce was pronounced in her favor. Nowadays, in most social circles, the decree absolute is coming to be looked upon as an absolution. I do not refer to the United States, where (I judge only from your novels) divorce outlaws nobody, but to steady old England, who still pretends that she frowns on the rebels and finally takes them back with a sigh and wonders what she is coming to. What England is coming to is to a lesser regard for the marriage bond, to a recognition that people have the right to rebel against their yoke. There totters the family--for marriage is its base, and the more English society receives in its ranks those who have flouted it, the more it will be shaken by the new spirit which bids human creatures live together, but also with the rest of the world. Woman was kept within the family by threats, by banishment, by ostracism, but now she easily earns forgiveness. At least English society is deciding to forget if it cannot forgive the guilt--a truly British expedient. At the root is a decaying respect for the marriage bond, a growing respect for rebellion. That tendency is everywhere, and it is becoming more and more common for husband and wife to take separate holidays; there are even some who leave behind them merely a slip: "Gone away, address unknown." They are cutting the wire entanglements behind which lie dangers and freedoms. All this again comes from mutual respect with mutual realization, from education, and especially from late marriages. Late marriages are one of the most potent causes of the break-up of the family, for now women are no longer caught and crushed young; they are no longer burdened matrons at thirty. The whole point of view has changed. I remember reading in an early-Victorian novel this phrase: "She was past the first bloom of her youth; she was twenty-three." The phrase is not without its meaning; it meant that the male was seeking not a wife, but a courtesan who, her courtesanship done, could become a perfect housekeeper. Now men prefer women of twenty-seven or twenty-eight, forsake the backfisch for her mother, because the mother has personality, experience, can stimulate, amuse, and accompany. Only the older and more formed woman is no longer willing to enter the family as a jail; she will enter it only as a hotel.

* * * * *

Meanwhile, from child to parent erosion also operates. I do not think that the modern child honors its father and its mother unless it thinks them worthy of honor. There is a slump in respect, as outside the family there is a slump in reverence. As in the outer world a man began by being a worthy, then a member of Parliament, then a minister, finally was granted a pension and later a statue; and as now a man is first a journalist, then a member of Parliament, a minister, and in due course a scoundrel, so inside the family does a father become an equal instead of a tyrant, and a good sort instead of an old fogy. For respect, I believe, was mainly fear and greed. The respect of the child for its father was very like the respect that Riquet, the little dog, felt for Monsieur Bergeret. Anatole France has expressed it ideally:

"Oh, my master, Bergeret, God of Slaughter, I worship thee! Hail, oh God of wrath! Hail, oh bountiful God! I lie at thy feet, I lick thy hand. Thou art great and beautiful when at the laden board thou devourest abundant meats. Thou art great and beautiful when, from a thin strip of wood causing flame to spring, thou dost of night make day...."

That was a little the child's cosmogony. Then the child became educated, capable of argument. In contact with more reasonable parents it grew more reasonable. The parent, confronted with the question, "Why must I do what you order?" ceased to say, "Because I say so." That reply did not seem good enough to the parent, and it ceased to be good enough for the child. If the child rebelled, the only thing to do was to strike it, and striking is no longer done; the parent prefers argument because the child is capable of understanding argument. The child is more lawful, more sensitive; it is unready to obey blindly, and it is no longer required to obey blindly, because, while the parent has begun to doubt his own infallibility, the child has been doing so, too. The child is more ready and more able to criticize its parents; indeed, the whole generation is critical, has acquired the habit of introspection. The child is a little like the supersoul of Mr. Stephen Leacock, and is developing thoughts like, "Why am I? Why am I what I am? How? and why how?" Obviously, such questions, when directed at one's father and mother, are a little shattering. It is true that once upon a time the child readily obeyed; now and then it criticized, but still it obeyed, for it had been told that its duty was to execute, as was its parents' to command. But duty is in a bad way, and I, for one, think that we should be well rid of duty, for it appears to me to be merely an excuse for acting without considering whether the deed is worthy. The man who dies for his country because he loves it is an idealist and a hero; the man who does that because he thinks it his duty is a fool. The conception of duty has suffered; from the child's point of view, it is almost extinct; it has been turned upside down, and there is a growth of opinion that the parent should have the duties and the child the privileges. It is the theory of La Course du Flambeau, where Hervieu shows us each generation using and bleeding the elder generation. Or perhaps it is a more subtle conception. It may be that the eugenic idea is vaguely forming in the young generation, and that, in an unperceived return to nature, they are deciding to eat their grandfathers, a primitive taste which I have never been able to understand. Youth, feeling that the world is its orange to suck, is inclined to consider that the elder generation, being responsible for its presence, should look after it and serve it. That is not at all illogical; it is borne out by Chinese law, where, if you save a man from suicide, you must feed him for the rest of his life.

Or perhaps it is a broader view, a more socialized one. Very young, the child is acquiring a vague sense of its responsibility to the race, is very early becoming a citizen. It is directed that way; it hears that liberty consists in doing what you like, providing you injure no other man. Its personality being encouraged to develop, the child acquires a higher opinion of itself, considers that it owes something to itself, that it has rights. Sacrifice is still inculcated in the child, but not so much because it is a moral duty as because it is mental discipline. The little boy is not told to give the chocolates to his little sister because she is a dear little thing, and he must not be cruel to her and make her cry; he is told that he must give her the chocolates because it is good for him to learn to give up something. That impulse is the impulse of Polycrates, who threw his ring into the sea. But, then, Polycrates had no luck. The child, more fortunate, is tending to realize itself as a person, and so, as it becomes more responsible, acquires tolerance; it makes allowances for its parents, it is kind, it realizes that its parents have not had its advantages. All that is very swollen-headed and unpleasant, but still I prefer it to the old attitude, to the time when voices were hushed and footsteps slowed when father's latchkey was heard in the lock. To the child the parent is becoming a person instead of the God of Wrath; a person with rights, but not a person to whom everything must be given up. Sacrifice is out of date, and in the child as well as in the elders there is a denial of the dream of Ellen Sturges Cooper, for few wake up and find that life is duty. My life, my personality--all that has sprung from Stirner, from Nietzsche, from the great modern reaction against socialism and uniformity; it is the assertion of the individual. It is often harsh; the daughter who used to take her father for a walk now sends the dog. But still it is necessary; old hens make good soup. I do not think that this has killed love, for love can coexist with mutual forbearance, however much Doctor Johnson may have doubted it. Doctor Johnson was the bad old man of the English family, and I do not suppose that anybody will agree that

"If the man who turnips cries Cry not when his father dies, 'Tis a proof that he had rather Have a turnip than his father."

A possible sentiment in an older generation, but sentiments, like generations, grow out of date; they are swept out by new ideas and new rejections--rejection of religion, rejection of morals. We tend toward an agnostic world, with a high philosophical morality; we have attained as yet neither agnosticism nor high morality, but the child is shaking off the ready-made precepts of the faiths and the Smilesian theories. It is unwillingly bound by the ordinances of a forgotten alien race; as a puling child, carried in a basket by an eagle, like the tiny builders of Ecbatana, it calls for bricks and mortar with which to build the airy castle of the future.

3

As a house divided against itself, the family falls. It protests, it hugs that from which it suffered; it protests in speech, in the newspapers, that still it is united. The clan is dead, and blood is not as thick as marmalade. There are countries where the link is strong, as in France, for instance. I quote from a recent and realistic novel the words of a mother speaking of her young married daughter:

"Every Tuesday we dine at my mother's, and every Thursday at my mother-in-law's. Of course, now, at least once a week we go to Madame de Castelac; later on I shall expect Pauline and her husband every Wednesday."

"That is a pity," said Sorel. "That leaves three days."

"Oh, there are other calls. Every week my mother comes to us the same evening as does my father-in-law, but that is quite informal."

Family dinners are rare in England. They flourish only at weddings and at funerals, especially at funerals, for mankind collected enjoys woe. But other occasions--birthdays, Christmas--are shunned; Christmas especially, in spite of Dickens and Mr. Chesterton, is not what it was, for its quondam victims, having fewer children, and being less bound to their aunts' apron strings, go away to the seaside, or stay at home and hide. That is a general change, and many modern factors, such as travel, intercourse with strangers, emigration, have shown the family that there are other places than home, until some of them have begun to think that "East or West, home's worst." There is a frigidity among the relations in the home, a disinclination to call one's mother-in-law "Mother." Indeed, relations-in-law are no longer relatives; the two families do not immediately after the wedding call one another Kitty or Tom. The acquired family is merely a sub-family, and often the grouping resembles that of the Montagues and the Capulets, if Romeo and Juliet had married. Mrs. Herbert said, charmingly, in Garden Oats, "Our in-laws are our strained relations."

With the closeness of the family goes the regard for the name, once so strong. I feel sure that in all seriousness, round about 1850, a father may have said to his son that he was disgracing the name of Smith. Now he may almost disgrace the name of FitzArundel for all anybody cares. There was a time when it was thought criminal that a man should become a bankrupt, but few families will now mortgage their estate to prevent a distant member's appearance before the official receiver. The name of the family is now merely generic, and the bold young girl of to-morrow will say, "My father began life as a forger and was ultimately hanged, but that shouldn't bother you, should it?" Much of that deliquescence is due to the factory system, for it opened opportunities to all, which many took, raised men high in the scale of wealth; one brother might be a millionaire in Manchester, while another tended a bar in Liverpool. Sometimes the rich member of the family came back, such as the uncle who returned from America with a fortune, in a state of sentimental generosity, but most of the time it has meant that the family split into those who keep their carriage and those who take the tram. Perhaps Cervantes did not exaggerate when saying that there are only two families: Have-Much and Have-Little.

4

What the future reserves I disincline to prophesy. It is enough to point to tendencies, and to say, "Along this road we go, we know not whither." But of one thing I feel certain: the family will not become closer, for the individualistic tendency of man leads to instinctive rebellion; his latent anarchism to isolate him from his fellows. There is a growing rebellion among women against the thrall of motherhood, which, however delightful it may be, is a thrall--the velvet-coated yoke is a yoke still. I do not suppose that the mothers of the future will unanimously deposit their babies in the municipality. But I do believe that with the growth of cooperative households, and especially of that quite new class, the skilled Princess Christian or Norland nurses, there will be a delegation of responsibility from the mother to the expert. It will go down to the poor as well as to the rich. Already we have district nurses for the poor, and I do not see why, as we realize more and more the value of young life, there should not be district kindergartens. They would remove the child still more from its home; they would throw it in contact with creatures of its own age in its very earliest years, prepare it for school, place it in an atmosphere where it must stand by itself among others who will praise or blame without special consideration, for they are strangers to it and do not bear its name.

I suspect, too, that marriage will be freer; it will not be made more easy or more difficult, but greater facilities will be given for divorce so that human beings may no longer be bound together in dislike, because they once committed the crime of loving unwisely. This, too, must loosen the family link, to-day still strong because people know that it is so hard to break it. It will be a conditional link when it can easily be done away with, a link that will be maintained only on terms of good behavior on both sides. The marriage service will need a new clause; we shall have to swear to be agreeable. The relation between husband and wife must change more. Conjugal tyranny still exists in a country such as England where the wife is not co-guardian of the child, for during his wife's lifetime a husband may remove her child into another country, refuse her access save at the price of a costly and uncertain legal action. The child itself must have rights. At present, all the rights it has are to such food as its parents will give it; it needs very gross cruelty before a man can be convicted of starving or neglecting his child. And when that child is what they call grown up--that is to say, sixteen--in practice it loses all its rights, must come out and fend for itself. I suspect that that will not last indefinitely, and that the new race will have upon the old race the claim that owing to the old race it was born. A socialized life is coming where there will be less freedom for those who are unfit to be free, those who do not feel categorical impulses, the impulse to treat wife and child gently and procure their happiness. Men will not indefinitely draw their pay on a Friday and drink half of it by Sunday night. Their wages will be subject to liens corresponding to the number of their children. These liens may not be light, and may extend long beyond the nominal majority of the child. I suspect that after sixteen, or some other early age, children will, if they choose, be entitled to leave home for some municipal hostel where for a while their parents will be compelled to pay for their support. It will be asked, "Why should a parent pay for the support of a child who will not live in his house?" It seems to me that the chief reply is, "Why did you have that child?" There is another, too: "By what right should this creature for whom you are responsible be tied to a house into which it has been called unconsulted? Why should it submit to your moral and religious views? to your friends? to your wall-paper?" It is a strong case, and I believe that, as time goes on and the law is strengthened, the young will more and more tend to leave their homes. In good, liberal homes they will stay, but the others they will abandon, and I believe that no social philosopher will regret that children should leave homes where they stay only because they are fed and not because they love.

So, flying apart by a sort of centrifugal force, the family will become looser and looser, until it exists only for those who care for one another enough to maintain the association. It cannot remain as it is, with its right of insult, its claim to society; we can have no more slave daughters and slave wives, nor shall we chain together people who spy out one another's loves and crush one another's youth. The family is immortal, but the immortals have many incarnations--from Pan and Bacchus sprang Lucifer, Son of the Morning. There is a time to come--better than this because it is to come--when the family, humanized, will be human.

VII

SOME NOTES ON MARRIAGE

1

The questioning mind, sole apparatus of the socio-psychologist, has of late years often concerned itself with marriage. Marriage always was discussed, long before Mrs. Mona Caird suggested in the respectable 'eighties that it might be a failure, but it is certain that with the coming of Mr. Bernard Shaw the institution which was questioned grew almost questionable. Indeed, marriage was so much attacked that it almost became popular, and some believe that the war may cut it free from the stake of martyrdom. Perhaps, but setting aside all prophecies, revolts and sermons, one thing does appear: marriage is on its trial before a hesitating jury. The judge has set this jury several questions: Is marriage a normal institution? Is it so normal as to deserve to continue in a state of civilization? given that civilization's function is to crush nature.

A thing is not necessarily good because it exists, for scarlet fever, nationality, art critics, and black beetles exist, yet all will be rooted out in the course of enlightenment. Marriage may be an invention of the male to secure himself a woman freehold, or, at least, in fee simple. It may be an invention of the female designed to secure a somewhat tyrannical protection and a precarious sustenance. Marriage may be afflicted with inherent diseases, with antiquity, with spiritual indigestion, or starvation: among these confusions the socio-psychologist, swaying between the solidities of polygamy and the shadows of theosophical union, loses all idea of the norm. There may be no norm, either in Christian marriage, polygamy, Meredithian marriage leases; there may be a norm only in the human aspiration to utility and to happiness.

For we know very little save the aimlessness of a life that may be paradise, or its vestibule, or an instalment of some other region. Still there is a key, no doubt: the will to happiness, which, alas! opens doors most often into empty rooms. It is the search for happiness that has envenomed marriage and made it so difficult to bear, because in the first rapture it is so hard to realize that there are no ways of living, but only ways of dying more or less agreeably.

Personally, I believe that with all its faults, with its crudity, its stupidity shot with pain, marriage responds to a human need to live together and to foster the species, and that though we will make it easier and approach free union, we shall always have something of the sort. And so, because I believe it eternal, I think it necessary.

But why does it fare so ill? Why is it that when we see in a restaurant a middle-aged couple, mutually interested and gay, we say: "I wonder if they are married?" Why do so many marriages persist when the love knot slips, and bandages fall away from the eyes? Strange cases come to my mind: M 6 and M 22, always apart, except to quarrel, meanly jealous, jealously mean, yet full of affability--to strangers; M 4 and many others, all poor, where at once the wife has decayed; when you see youth struggling in vain on the features under the cheap hat, you need not look at the left hand: she is married. It is true that however much they may decay in pride of body and pride of life, when all allowances are made for outer gaiety and grace, the married of forty are a sounder, deeper folk than their celibate contemporaries. Often bled white by self-sacrifice, they have always learnt a little of the world's lesson, which is to know how to live without happiness. They may have been vampires, but they have not gone to sleep in the cotton wool of their celibacy. Even hateful, the other sex has meant something to them. It has meant that the woman must hush the children because father has come home, but it has also meant that she must change her frock, because even father is a man. It has taught the man that there are flowers in the world, which so few bachelors know; it has taught the woman to interest herself in something more than a fried egg, if only to win the favor of her lord. Marriage may not teach the wish to please, but it teaches the avoidance of offence, which, in a civilization governed by negative commandments, is the root of private citizenship.

2

For the closer examination of the marriage problem, I am considering altogether one hundred and fifty cases; my acquaintance with them varies between intimate and slight. I have thrown out one hundred and sixteen cases where the evidence is inadequate: the following are therefore not loose generalizations, but one thing I assert: those one hundred and sixteen cases do not contain a successful marriage. Out of the remaining thirty-four, the following results arise:

Apparently successful 9 Husband unfaithful 5 Wife unfaithful 10 Husband dislikes wife 3 Wife dislikes husband 7

Success is a vague word, and I attempt no definition, but we know a happy marriage when we see it, as we do a work of art.

It should be observed that when one or both parties are unfaithful, the marriage is not always unsuccessful, but it generally is; moreover, there are difficulties in establishing proportion, for women are infinitely more confidential on this subject than are men; they also frequently exaggerate dislike, which men cloak in indifference. Still, making all these allowances, I am unable to find more than nine cases of success, say six per cent. This percentage gives rise to platitudinous thoughts on the horrid gamble of life.

Two main conclusions appear to follow: that more wives than husbands break their marriage vows, and (this may be a cause as well as an effect) that more wives than husbands are disappointed in their hopes. This is natural enough, as nearly all women come ignorant to a state requiring cool knowledge and armored only with illusion against truth, while men enter it with experience, if not with tolerance born of disappointment. I realize that these two conclusions are opposed to the popular belief that a good home and a child or two are enough to make a woman content. (A bad home and a child or nine is not considered by the popular mind.)

There is no male clamor against marriage, from which one might conclude that man is fairly well served. No doubt he attaches less weight to the link; even love matters to him less than to women. I do not want to exaggerate, for Romeo is a peer to Juliet, but it is possible to conceive Romeo on the Stock Exchange, very busy in pursuit of money and rank, while Juliet would remain merely Juliet. Juliet is not on the Stock Exchange. If business is good, she has nothing to do, and if Satan does not turn her hands to evil works, he may turn them to good ones, which will not improve matters very much. Juliet, idle, can do nothing but seek a deep and satisfying love: mostly it is a lifelong occupation. All this makes Juliet very difficult, and no astronomer will give her the moon.

Romeo is in better plight, for he makes less demands. Let Juliet be a good housekeeper, fairly good looking and good tempered; not too stupid, so as to understand him; not too clever, so that he may understand her; such that he may think her as good as other men's wives, and he is satisfied. The sentimental business is done; it is "Farewell! Farewell! ye lovely young girls, we're off to Rio Bay." So to work--to money--to ambition--to sport--to anything--but Juliet. While he forgets her, the modern woman grows every day more attractive, more intellectually vivid. She demands of her partner that he should give her stimulants, and he gives her soporifics. She asks him for far too much; she is cruel, she is unjust, and she is magnificent. She has not the many children on whom in simpler days her mother used to vent an exacting affection, so she vents it on her husband.

Yet it is not at first sight evident why so easily in England a lover turns into a husband, that is to say, into a vaguely disagreeable person who can be coaxed into paying bills. I suspect there are many influences corrupting marriage, and most of them are mutual in their action; they are of the essence of the contract; they are the mental reservations of the marriage oath. So far as I can see, they fall into sixteen classes:--

1. The waning of physical attraction. 2. Diverging tastes. 3. Being too much together. 4. Being too much apart. (There is no pleasing this institution.) 5. The sense of mutual property. 6. The sense of the irremediable. 7. Children. 8.

The cost of living. 9. Rivalry. 10. Polygamy in men and "second blooming" in women. 11. Coarseness and talkativeness. 12. Sulkiness. 13. Dull lives. 14. Petty intolerance. 15. Stupidity. 16. Humour and aggressiveness.

There are other influences, but they are not easily ascertained; sometimes they are subtle.

M 28 said to me: "My husband's grievance against me is that I have a cook who can't cook; my grievance against him is that he married me."

Indeed, sentiment and the scullery painfully represent the divergence of the two sexes. One should not exaggerate the scullery; the philosopher who said "Feed the brute" was not entirely wrong, but it is quite easy for a woman to ignore the emotional pabulum that many a man requires. It is quite true that "the lover in the husband may be lost", but very few women realize that the wife can blot out the mistress. Case M 19 confessed that she always wore out her old clothes at home, and she was surprised when I suggested that though her husband was no critic of clothes, he might often wonder why she did not look as well as other women. Many modern wives know this; in them the desire to please never quite dies; between lovers, it is violent and continuous; between husband and wife, it is sometimes maintained only by shame and self-respect: there are old slippers that one can't wear, even before one's husband.

The problem arises very early with the waning of physical attraction. I am not thinking only of the bad and hasty marriages so frequent in young America, but of the English marriages, where both parties come together in a state of sentimental excitement born of ignorance and rather puritanical restraint. Europeans wed less wisely than the Hindoo and the Turk, for these realize their wives as Woman. Generally they have never seen a woman of their own class, and so she is a revelation, she is indeed the bulbul, while he, being the first, is the King of men. But the Europeans have mixed too freely, they have skimmed, they have flirted, they have been so ashamed of true emotion that they have made the Song of Solomon into a vaudeville ditty. They have watered the wine of life.

So when at last the wine of life is poured out, the draught is not new, for they have quaffed before many an adulterated potion and have long pretended that the wine of life is milk. For a moment there is a difference, and they recognize that the incredible can happen; each thinks the time has come:

"Wenn ich dem Augenblick werd sagen: Verweile doch, du bist so sch 辣 . . ."

Then the false exaltation subsides: not even a saint could stand a daily revelation; the revelation becomes a sacramental service, the sacramental service a routine, and then, little by little, there is nothing. But nature, as usual abhorring a vacuum, does not allow the newly opened eyes to dwell upon a void; it leaves them clear, it allows them to compare. One day two demi-gods gaze into the eyes of two mortals and resent their fugitive quality. Another day two mortals gaze into the eyes of two others, whom suddenly they discover to be demi-gods. Some resist the trickery of nature, some succumb, some are fortunate, some are strong. But the two who once were united are divorced by the three judges of the Human Supreme Court: Contrast, Habit, and Change.

Time cures no ills; sometimes it provides poultices, often salt, for wounds. Time gives man his work, which he always had, but did not realize in the days of his enchantment; but to woman time seldom offers anything except her old drug, love. Oh! there are other things, children, visiting cards, frocks, skating rinks, Christian Science teas, and Saturday anagrams, but all these are but froth. Brilliant, worldly, hard-eyed, urgent, pleasure-drugged, she still believes there is an exquisite reply to the question:

"Will the love you are so rich in Light a fire in the kitchen, And will the little God of Love turn the spit, spit, spit?"

Only the little God of Love does not call, and the butcher does.

It is her own fault. It is always one's own fault when one has illusions, though it is, in a way, one's privilege. She is attracted to a strange man because he is tall and beautiful, or short and ugly and has a clever head, or looks like a barber; he comes of different stock, from another country, out of another class--and these two strangers suddenly attempt to blend a total of, say, fifty-five years of different lives into a single one! Gold will melt, but it needs a very fierce fire, and as soon as the fire is withdrawn, it hardens again. Seldom is there anything to make it fluid once more, for the attraction, once primary, grows with habit commonplace, with contrast unsatisfactory, with growth unsuitable. The lovers are twenty, then in love, then old.

It is true that habit affects man not in the same way as it does woman; after conquest man seems to grow indifferent, while, curiously enough, habit often binds woman closer to man, breeds in her one single fierce desire: to make him love her more. Man buys cash down, woman on the instalment plan, horribly suspecting now and then that she is really buying on the hire system. A rather literary case, Case M 11, said to me: "I am much more in love with him than I was in the beginning; he seemed so strange and hard then. Now I love him, but ... he seems tired of me; he knows me too well. I wonder whether we only fall in love with men just about the time that they get sick of us."

Her surmise may be correct: there is no record of the after-life of Perseus and Andromeda, and it is more romantic not to delve into it. Neither they nor any other lovers could hope to maintain the early exaltations. I am reminded of a well-known picture by Mr. Charles Dana Gibson, showing two lovers in the snow by the sea. They are gazing into each other's eyes; below is written: "They began saying good-by last summer." Does any one doubt that a visit to the minister, say, in the autumn, might have altered the complexion of things? And no wonder, for they were the unknown, and through marriage would become the known. It is only the unknown that tempts, until one realizes that the unknown and the known are the same thing, as Socrates realized that life and death are the same thing, mere converses of a single proposition. It is the unknown makes strange associates, attracts men to ugly women, slatterns to dandies. It is not only contrast, it is the suspicion that the unexpected outside must conceal something. The breaking down of that concealment is conquest, and after marriage there is no conquest; there is only security: who could live dangerously in Brooklyn? Once licensed, love is official; its gifts are doled out as sugar by a grocer, and sometimes short weighed. Men suffer from this and many go dully wondering what it is they miss that once they had; they go rather heavy, rather dense, cumbrously gallant, asking to be understood, and whimpering about it in a way that would be ridiculous if it were not a little pathetic. Meanwhile, their wives wonder why all is not as it was. It is no use telling them that nothing can ever be as it was, that as mankind by living decays, the emotions and outlook must change; to have had a delight is a deadly thing, for one wants it again, just as it was, as a child demands always the same story. It must be the same delight, and none who feel emotion will ever understand that "the race of delights is short and pleasures have mutable faces."

It is true that early joys may unite, especially if one can believe that there is only one fountain of joy. I think of many cases,--M 5, M 33,--where there is only one cry: "It is cruel to have had delights, for the glamour of the past makes the day darker." They will live to see the past differently when they are older and the present matters less. But until then, the dead joy poisons the animate present; the man must drift away to his occupation, for there is nothing else, and the woman must harden by wanting what she cannot have. She will part herself from him more thoroughly by hardening, for one cannot count upon a woman's softness; it can swiftly be transmuted into malicious hatred.

3

This picture of pain is the rule where two strangers wed, but there are some who, taking a partner discover a friend, many who develop agreeable acquaintanceship. Passion may be diverted into a common interest, say in conchology; if people are not too stupid, not too egotistic, they very soon discover in each other a little of the human good will that will not die. They must, or they fail. For whereas in the beginning foolish lips may be kissed, a little later they must learn to speak some wisdom. In this men are most exacting; they are most inclined to demand that women should hold up to their faces the mirror of flattery, while women seem more tolerant, often because they do not understand, very often because they do not care, and echo the last words of Mr. Bernard Shaw's Ann: "Never mind her, dear, go on talking;" perhaps because they have had to tolerate so much in the centuries that they have grown expert. One may, however, tolerate whilst strongly disapproving, and one must disapprove when one's egotism is continually insulted by the other party's egotism. There is very little room for twice "I" in what ought to have been "We", and we nearly all feel that the axis of the earth passes through our bodies. So the common interests of two egotisms can alone make of these one egotism. The veriest trifle will serve, and pray do not smile at Case M 4, who forgive each other all wrongs when they find for dinner a risotto ?la Milanaise. A slightly spasmodic interest, and one not to be compared with a common taste for golf, or motoring, or entertaining, but still it is not to be despised. It is so difficult to pick a double interest from the welter of things that people do alone; it is so difficult for wives truly to sympathize with games, business, politics, newspapers, inventions; most women hate all that. And it is still more difficult, just because man is man and master, for him really to care for the fashions, for gossip, for his wife's school friends, and especially her relations, for tea parties, tennis tournaments at the Rectory, lectures at the Mutual Improvement Association, servants' misdeeds, and growths in the garden. Most men hate all that. People hold amazing conversations:

She: "Do you know, dear, I saw Mrs. Johnson again to-day with that man."

He: (Trying hard) "Oh! yes, the actor fellow, you mean."

She: (Reproachfully) "No, of course not, I never said he was an actor. He's the new engineer at the mine, the one who came from Mexico."

He: "Oh! yes, that reminds me, did you go to the library and get me Roosevelt's book on the Amazon?"

She: "No dear, I'm sorry I forgot. You see I had such a busy day, and I couldn't make up my mind between those two hats. The very big one and the very small one. You know. Now tell me what you really think--" and so on.

It is exactly like a Tchekoff play. They make desperate efforts to be interested in each other's affairs, and sometimes they succeed, for they manage to stand each other's dullness. They assert their egotism in turns. He tells the same stories several times. He takes her for a country walk and forgets to give her tea, and she never remembers that he hates her dearest friend Mabel. Where the rift grows more profound is when trifles such as these are overlooked, and particularly where a man has work that he loves, or to which he is used, which is much the same thing. In early days the woman's attitude to a man's work varies a good deal, but she generally suspects it a little. She may tolerate it because she loves him, and all that is his is noble. Later, if this work is very profitable, or if it is work which leads to honour, she may take a pride in it, but even then she will generally grudge it the time and the energy it costs. She loves him, not his work. She will seldom confess this, even to herself, but she will generally lay down two commandments:

1. Thou shalt love me.

2. Thou shalt succeed so that I may love thee.

All this is not manifest, but it is there. It is there even in the days of courtship, when a man's work, a man's clothes, a man's views on bimetallism are sacred; in those days, the woman must kowtow to the man's work, just as he must keep on good terms with her pet dog. But the time almost invariably comes when the man kicks the pet dog, because pet dogs are madly irritating sometimes--and so is a man's work. There is something self-protective in this, for work is so domineering. I should not be at all surprised to hear that Galatea saw to it that Pygmalion never made another statue. (On second thoughts it strikes me that there might be other reasons for that.)

It is true that Pygmalion was an artist, and these are proverbially difficult husbands: after an hour's work an artist will "sneer, backbite and speak daggers." Art is a vampire, and it will gladly gobble up a wife as well as a husband, but the wife must not do any gobbling. She does not always try to, and there are many in London who follow their artist husbands rather like sandwichmen between two boards, but they are of a trampled breed, indigenous, I suspect, to England. I think they arise but little in America, where, as an American said to me, "women labor to advance themselves along a road paved with discarded husbands." (This is an American's statement, not mine, so I ask the Reverend John Bootfeller, President of the Kansas and Nevada Society for the Propagation of the Intellect, to spare me his denunciations.)

But leaving aside such important things as personal pettinesses, which too few think important, it must be acknowledged that women seldom conceive the passion for art that can inflame a man. They very seldom conceive a passion for anything except passion,--an admirable tendency for which they blush as one does for all one's natural manifestations. They hardly ever care for philosophy; they generally hate politics, but they nearly always love votes. They are quite as irritating in that way as men, who almost invariably adore politics and detest realities, sometimes love science and generally prefer record railway runs. But where such an interest as a science or an art has reigned supreme in a man, and reasserts itself after marriage, she recognizes her enemy, the serpent, for is he not the symbol of wisdom? Invariably he rears his head when the love fever has subsided. Woman's impulse is more artistic than man's, but it seldom touches art; her artistic impulse is not yet one of high grade; she is the flower arranger rather than the flower painter, the flower painter rather than just the painter. But this instinct that is in all women and in so few men avails just enough to make them discontented, while the great instinct that is in a few men is always enough to make them wretched.

It would not be so bad if they had not to live together, but social custom has decided that couples must forsake their separate ways and evermore follow the same. Most follow the common path easily enough, because most follow the first path that offers, but many grumble and cast longing eyes at side tracks or would return to the place whence they came. They cannot do so because it is not done, because other feet have not broken paths so wide that they shall seem legitimate. When husband and wife care no longer for their common life, the only remedy is to part: then the contradictory strain that is in all of us will reassert itself and make them rebound towards each other. If the law were to edict that man and wife should never be together for more than six months in the year, it would be broken every day, and men and women would stand hunger and stripes to come together for twelve months in twelve. If love of home were made a crime, a family life would arise more touching than anything Queen Victoria ever dreamed. But from the point of view of a barbarous present, this would never do, for the very worst that can happen to two people is to reach the fullness of their desire. The young man who raves at the young woman's feet: "Oh! that I were by your side day and night! Oh! that ever I could watch you move! I grudge the night the eight hours in which you sleep!"-- Well, that young man is generally successful in his wooing and gets what he wants; a little later he gets a little more. For proximity is a dangerous thing; it enables one to know another rather well: full knowledge of mankind is seldom edifying. One sees too much, one sees too close; a professional Don Juan who honors me with his friendship told me that he has an infallible remedy against falling in love more often than three times a day: "Stand as close to your charmer as you can, look at her well, very well, at every feature; watch her attitudes, listen to every tone of her voice;

then you will discover something unpleasant, and you will be saved." That is a little what happens in marriage; for ever and ever people are together, hearing each other, watching each other. Listen to M 14:

"I really was very much in love with him and only just at the end of the engagement did I notice how hard he blew his nose. After we were married, I thought: 'Oh! don't be so silly and notice such little things, he's such a splendid fellow.' A little later--'Oh! I do wish he wouldn't blow his nose like that, it drives me mad.' Now I find myself listening and telling myself with an awful feeling of doom: 'He's going to blow his nose!'"

(She never tells him that he trumpets like an elephant. She fears to offend him. She prefers to stand there, exasperated and chafed. One day he will trumpet down the walls of her Jericho.)

There are awful little things between two people. Here are some of them:

M 43. When tired, the wife has a peculiar yawn, roughly: "Hoo-hoo! Hoo-hoo!" The husband hears it coming, and something curls within him.

M 98. Every morning in his bath the husband sings: "There is a fountain fill'd with blood drawn from Emmanuel's veins," always the same.

M 124. The wife buys shoes a quarter size too small and always slips them off under the table at dinner. Then she loses them and develops great agitation. This fills her husband with an unaccountable rage.

M 68. The wife is afflicted with the clich?habit and can generally sum up a situation by phrases such as: "All is not gold that glitters." Or, "Such is life." Or, "Well, well, it's a weary world." The husband can hear them coming.

There are scores of these little cruel things which wear away love as surely as trickling water will wear away a stone. (Observe how contagious clich 閦 are!) The dilemma is horrible; if the offended party speaks out, he or she may speak out much too forcibly and raise this sort of train of thought: "He didn't seem to mind when we were engaged. He loved me then, and little things didn't matter. He doesn't love me now. I wonder whether he is in love with some one else. Oh! I'm so unhappy." If, on the other hand, one does not speak out forcibly, or does not speak at all, the offender goes on doing it for the rest of his or her life, and there is nothing to do except to wait until one has got used to it and has ceased to care. But by that time one has generally ceased to care for the offender.

There are ideal marriages where both parties aim at perfection and are willing to accept mutual criticism. But there is something a little callous in this form of self-improvement society. People who are too much together are always making notes, adding up in their hearts bitter little adverse balances with which they will one day confront the fallen lover. Some slight offense will bring up the bill of arrears. A quarrel about a forgotten ticket will give life to the cruel thing he said seven years before about her mother's bonnets, or her sudden dismissal of the cook, or the dreadful day when he sat on the eggs in the train. (Clumsy brute!) All these things pile up and pile up until they form a terrible, towering cairn made up of tiny stones, but of great total weight, just as an avalanche rests securely upon a crest until a whisper releases it. Nearly all marriages are in a state of permanent mobilization. There is only one thing to do, to remember all the time that one could not hope to meet one quite great enough to be one's mate, and that this is the best the world can do. The thought that nobody can quite understand one or quite appreciate one arouses a delicious sorrow and an enormous pride.

4

Too much together is bad, and too much apart may be worse. As I suggested before, there is no pleasing this institution.

It is easier to live too separate than too close, for one comes together freshly, and marriage feels less irremediable when it hardly exists. There really are couples who care for each other very well, who meet in a country house and say: "What! you here! How jolly!" That is an extreme case. In practice, separateness means conjugal acquaintanceship. Different pleasures, different friends, perhaps different worlds; indeed, one is mutually fresh, but traveling different roads, one may find that there is nothing in common. Of two evils, it is better perhaps to be too intimate than too distant, because there are many irritating things that with reminiscence become delightful. The dreadful day when he sat on the eggs in the train is not entirely dreadful, for he looked so silly when he stood up, removing the eggs, and though one was angry, one vaguely loved him for having made a fool of himself. (There are nine and sixty ways of gaining affection, and one of them is to be a good-tempered butt.)

Separateness, naturally, cannot coincide with the sense of mutual property. This is perhaps the cause of the greatest unhappiness in marriage, for so many forget that to be married is not to be one. They do not understand that however much they may love, whatever delights they may share, whatever common ambitions they may harbor, whatever they hope, or endeavor, or pray, two people are still two people. Or if they know it, they say, "He is mine." "She is mine." If one could give oneself entirely, it would be well enough, but however much one may want to do so one cannot, just because one is the axis of the earth. Because one cannot, one will not, and he that would absorb will never forgive. He will be jealous, he will be suspicious, tyrannical, he will watch and lay traps, he will court injury, he will air grievances, because the next best thing to complete possession is railing at his impotency to conquer. That jealousy is turned against everything, against work, against art, against relatives, friends, dead loves, little children, toy dogs: "Thou shalt have none other gods but me" is a human commandment.

Men do not, as a rule, suffer very much from this desire to possess, because they are so sure that they do possess, because they find it so difficult to conceive that their wife can find any other man attractive. They are too well accustomed to being courted, even if they are old and repulsive, because they have power and money; only they think it is because they are men. Beyond a jealous care for their wives' fidelity, which I suspect arises mainly from the feeling that an unfaithful wife is a criticism, they do not ask very much. But women suffer more deeply because they know that man has lavished on them for centuries a condescending admiration, that the king who lays his crown at their feet knows that his is the crown to give. While men possess by right of possession, women possess only by right of precarious conquest. They feel it very bitterly, this fugitive empire, and their greatest tragedy is to find themselves growing a little older, uncertain of their power, for they know they have only one power; they are afraid, as age comes, of losing their man, while I have never heard of a husband afraid of losing his wife, or able to repress his surprise if she forsook him.

It would not matter so much if the feeling of property were that of a good landlord, who likes to see his property develop and grow beautiful, but mutual property is the feeling of the slave owner. Sometimes both parties suffer so, and by asking too much lose all. Man seldom asks much: if only a wife will not compromise his reputation for attractiveness while maintaining her own by flirtation, if she will accept his political views, acquire a taste for his favorite holiday resorts, and generally say, "Yes, darling", or "No, darling", opportunely, she need do nothing, she has only "beautifully to be." He is not so fortunate, however, when she wants to possess him, for she demands that he should be active, that the pretty words, caresses, the anxious inquiries after health, the presents of flowers and of stalls should continue. It is not enough that he should love her; he must still be her lover. When she is not sure that he still is her lover, a madness of unrest comes over her; she will lacerate him, she will invent wishes so that he may thwart them, she will demand his society when she knows it is mortgaged to another occupation, so that she may suffer his refusal, exaggerate his indifference. Here are cases:

M 21. She: "He used to take me to dances. The other day he wouldn't come, he said he was tired. He wasn't tired when we were engaged."

The Investigator: "But why should he go if he didn't want to?"

She: "Because I wanted to."

The Investigator: "But he didn't want to."

She: "He ought to take pleasure in pleasing me."

(The conversation here degenerates into a discussion on duty and becomes uninteresting.)

M 4. The husband is a doctor with a very extended city practice. He is busy eleven hours a day and has night calls. His marriage has been spoilt because in the first years the wife, who is young and gay, could not understand that the man, who was always surrounded by people, in houses, streets, conveyances, should not desire society. She resented his wish to be alone for some hours, to shut himself up. There were tears, and like most people she looked ugly when she cried. She was lonely, and when one is lonely, it is difficult to realize that other people may be too much surrounded.

5

A great deal of all this, however, might pass away if one could feel that it would not last. Nothing matters that does not last. Only one must be conscious of it, and in marriage many people are dully aware that they have settled down, that they have drawn the one and only ticket they can ever hope to draw, unless merciful death steps in. There will be no more adventures, no more excitements, no more marsh fires, which one knows deceptive yet loves to follow. It will be difficult to move to other towns or countries, to change one's occupation; it will even be difficult to adopt new poses, for the other will not be taken in. One will be for evermore what one is. True there is elopement, divorce; in matters of art, there is the artist courage that enables a man to see another suffer for the sake of his desire. But all this is very difficult, and few of us have courage enough to make others suffer; if one had the courage to do no harm at all, it might not be so bad, but not many can follow Mr. Bernard Shaw: "If you injure your neighbor, let it not be by halves." They almost invariably do injure by halves: he that will not kill, scratches. There is no refuge from a world of rates, and taxes, and bills, and houses overcrowded by children, and old clothes, dull leaders in the papers, stupid plays, the morning train, the unvarying Sunday dinner. It is so bad sometimes that it causes willful revolt. I sincerely believe that a great many men would be model husbands if only they were not married. Only when everything is respectable and nice there is a terrible temptation to introduce a change; the wild animal in man, that is in a few a lion, in most a weasel, reacts against the definite, the irremediable, the assured. He must do something. He must break through. He must prove to himself that he has not really sentenced himself to penal servitude for life. That is why so few of the respectable are respectable, and why reformed rakes do make good husbands. (Generally, that is, for a few rakes feel that they must keep up their reputation; on the other hand, a really respectable man knows no shame.)

Curiously enough, children seem to act both against and in favor of these disruptive factors. It is difficult to deprive children of influence; they must part, or they must unite. They are somebody in the house; they make a noise, and it depends upon temperament whether the noise exasperates or delights. Parents are divided into those who love them, and those who bear their children; generally, men dislike little babies, unless they are rather strong men whom weakness attracts, or unless they feel pride of race, while women, excepting those who live only for light pleasures, give them a quite unreasoning affection. Children are a frequent source of trouble, for the tired man's nerves are horribly frayed by screams and exuberances. He shouts: "Stop that child howling!" and if his wife assumes a saintly air and says that "she would rather hear a child cry than a man swear," the door opens towards the club or public house. Likewise, a man who has given so many jewels that the mother of the Gracchi might be jealous, will never understand the appalling weariness that can come over the mother in the evening, when she has administered, say, twelve meals, four or eight baths, and answered several hundreds of questions varying between the existence of God and the esoterics of the steam engine. Loving the children too much to blame them, she must blame some one, and blames him.

People do not confess these things, but the socio-psychologist must remember that when a man quietly picks up a flower pot and hurls it through the window, the original cause may be found in the behavior of the departmental manager six hours before. The irritation of children can envenom two lives, for it seems almost inevitable that each party should think the other spoils or tyrannizes. It is not always so, and sometimes children unite by the bond of a common love; very much more often they unite by the burden of a common responsibility. Indeed, it is this financial responsibility that draws two people close, because tied together they must swim together or sink together, until they are so concerned individually with their salvation that they think they are concerned with the salvation of the other. That bond of union is dangerous, because marriage is expensive, and because one tends to remember the time when bread was not so dear and flesh and blood so cheap. There is affluence in bachelordom; there is atrocious discomfort too, but when one thinks of the good old times, one generally forgets all except the affluence. Of the present, one sees only that one cannot take the whole family to Yellowstone; of the past, one does not see the sitting room, or the hangings on which the landlady merely blew. The wife thinks of her frocks, garlands of the sacrificial heifer, the husband of the days when he could afford to be one of the boys. And, as soon as the past grows glamorous, the present day grows dull; always because one must blame something, one blames the other. It is so much more agreeable to spend a thousand dollars than to spend a hundred, even if one gets nothing for it. It is power. It is excitement. One thinks of money until one may come to think of nothing but money, until, as suggested before, a husband turns into a vaguely disagreeable person who can be coaxed into paying bills. In the working class especially there is bitterness among the women, who before their marriage knew the taste of independence and of earned money in their purses. It is a great love that can compensate a woman for the loss of freedom after she has enjoyed it.

Nothing indeed can compensate a woman for this, except a lover, that is to say, a return to an older state. That is to what she turns, for strange as it may seem, marriage does not vaccinate against the temptations of love. She does not easily love again, for she has been married, and while it is easy to love again when one has been atrociously betrayed, just because one invests the new with everything that the old held back, it is difficult to love again when the promised love turned merely to dullness. There is nothing to strike against. There is no contrast, and so women slip into relationships that are silly, because there is nothing real behind them. Boredom is the root of all evil, and I doubt whether busy and happy women seek adventure, for few of them want it for adventure's sake: they seek only satisfaction. That is what most men cruelly misunderstand; they blame woman instead of searching out their own remissness. Sins of omission matter more than sins of commission, more even than infidelities, for love, which is all a woman's life, is only a momentous incident in that of a man. Love may be the discovery of a happiness, but man remains conscious of many other delights. Woman is seldom like that. You will imagine a man and a woman who have blundered upon mutual understanding standing upon the hill from which Moses saw Canaan. The woman would fill her eyes with Canaan, and could see nought else, while the man gazing at the promised land would still be conscious of other countries. In the heart of a man who is worth anything at all, love must have rivals,--art, science, ambition,--and it is a delight to woman that there should be rivals to overcome, even though it be a poor slave she tie to her chariot wheels.

Marriage does not always suffer when people drift away from their allegiance; in countries such as France notably, where many husbands and wives do not think it necessary to trust, or tactful to watch each other, the problem does not set itself so sharply. It is mainly in Anglo-Saxon countries where the little blue flower has its altars that the trouble begins. A rather fascinating foreigner said to me once: "Englishwomen are very troublesome;

they are either so light that they do not understand you when you tell them you love them, or so deep that you must elope every time. This is a difficult country." I do not want to seem cynical, but the polygamous nature of man is so ill-recognized and the boredom of woman such a national institution that when it is too late to pretend that that which has happened has not happened, most of the mischief has already been done. Why a husband or wife who has found attraction in another should immediately treat his partner abominably is not easily understood, for falling in love with the present victim need not make him rude or remiss to the rest of the world. But the British are a strange and savage people. Also, when in doubt they get drunk, so I fear I must leave a clearer recognition of polygamous instincts to the slow-growing enlightenment of the mind of man.

He is growing enlightened; at least he is infinitely more educated than he was, for he has begun to recognize that woman is to a certain extent a human being, a savage, a barbarian, but entitled to the consideration generally given to the Hottentot. I do not think woman will always be savage, though I hope she will not turn into the clear-eyed, weather-beaten mate that Mr. H. G. Wells likes to think of--for the future. She has come to look upon man as an equation that can be solved. He, too, in a sense, and both are to-day much less inclined than they were fifty years ago to overlook a chance of pleasing. It is certain that men and women to-day dress more deliberately for each other than they ever did before, that they lead each other, sometimes with dutiful unwillingness, to the theatre or the country; it is very painful sometimes, this organization of pleasure, but it is necessary because dull lives are bad lives, and better fall into the river than never go to the river at all. It is dangerous and vain to take up the attitude, "I alone am enough." Yet many do: as one walks along a suburban street, where every window is shut, where every dining room has its aspidistra in a pot, one realizes that scores of people are busily heaping ash upon the once warm fire of their love. The stranger is the alternative; he obscures small quarrels; if the stranger is beautiful, he urges to competition; if he is inferior, he soothes pride. But above all, the stranger is change, therefore hope. The stranger is an insurance against loss of personal pride; he compels adornment, for what is "good enough for my husband" is not good enough for the lady over the way. The stranger serves the pleasure lust, this violent passion of man, and cannot harm him because the lust for pleasure, within the limits of hysteria, involves a desire for good looks, for elegance, for gaiety; above all, love of pleasure was reviled of our fathers, and whatever our fathers thought bad is become a good thing. Our fathers did not understand certain forms of pride: there is more than pride of body in good looks, good clothes, and showing off before acquaintances: there is achievement, which means pride of conquest. I imagine that the happiest couple in the world is the one where each lives in perpetual fear that somebody will run away with the other.

Looking at it broadly, I see marriage as a Chinese puzzle, almost, but not quite, insoluble. Spoilt by coldness, spoilt by ardour, spoilt by excess, spoilt by indifference, spoilt by obedience, by stupidity, by self-assertion, spoilt by familiarity, spoilt by ignorance. Spoilt in every possible way that man can invent. Spoilt by every ounce of influence a jealous or ironical world can muster, spoilt by habit, by contrast, by obtuseness quite as much as by overclose understanding. And yet it stands. It stands because there is nothing much to put into its place, because marriage is the only road that leads a man away from his dinner when he is forty-five, or teaches a woman to preserve her complexion. It stands like most human things, because it is the better of two bad alternatives. Only because it stands we must not think that it will never change. All things change, otherwise one could not bear them. I suspect that marriage, that was once upon a time the taking of a woman by a man, which has now grown legalized, and may become courteous, will turn into a very skilled occupation. It will be recognized still more than now that all freedom need not be lost after putting on the wedding ring. As legal right and privilege grow, as women develop private earnings, a consciousness of worth must arise. Already women realize their value and demand its recognition. If they demand it long enough, they will get it. I suspect that the economic problem is at the root of the marriage problem, for people are not indiscriminate in their relationships, and even Don Juan, after a while, longs to be faithful, if only somebody could teach him how to be it. Marriage can be made close only by making divorce easy, by extending female labor. For labor makes woman less attractive and to be attractive is rather a trap: how much higher can a woman rise? But the economic freedom of woman will mean that she need not bind herself; she will be able to break away, and in those days she will be most completely bound, for who would run away from a jail if the door were always left open?

I detest Utopia, and these things seem so far away that I am more content to take marriage as it is in the hope that unhealthy novels, unnecessary discussions, unwholesome views, and unnatural feelings may little by little reform mankind. Meanwhile, I hold fast to the private maxim that hardly anything is unendurable if one sets up that all mankind could not give one a quite worthy mate. But there is another alleviation: understanding not only that one is married to somebody else, but also that somebody else is married to yourself, and that it is quite as hard for the other party. There are many excellent things to be done; here are a few:

(1) Do not open each other's letters. (For one reason you might not like the contents.) And try not to look liberal if you don't even glance at the address or the postmark.

(2) Vary your pursuits, your conversation, and your clothes. If required, vary your hair.

(3) If you absolutely must be sincere, let it be in private.

(4) (Especially for wives.) Find out on the honeymoon whether crying or swearing is the more effective.

(5) Once a day say to a wife: "I love you"; to a husband: "How strong you are!" If the latter remark is ridiculous, say: "How clever you are!" for everybody believes that.

(6) Forgive your partner seventy times seven. Then burn the ledger.

###

www.ingramcontent.com/pod-product-compliance
Lightning Source LLC
Chambersburg PA
CBHW072248310526
45795CB00011B/444